Photo by: Chelsie Hutto

Tribute to Paula Ramsey
"Mom"

    Paula Ramsey, founder & owner of "A Lady's Day Out" has gone to be with her sweet savior. On August 22, 2000 she lost her battle with cancer. Mom's life was an example for many. We can all be assured her rewards were great and that the Father welcomed her home with open arms and a big "Thank you" for a life spent glorifying Him and bringing many into the Kingdom.

    "A Lady's Day Out" was Mom's vision. As with most things in her life, she was willing to share this with me. We traveled from one exciting town to the next—finding treasures and experiencing so much together for more than 10 years. I was blessed to have shared these times with my mom and hold them dear in the quiet places of my heart.

    The loss of my best friend, business partner and mother is great, and the pain is deep. Our family has lost our "rock," but our faith in the Lord is strong, and we take comfort in knowing we will someday join her again in heaven.

I will miss our adventures together, but I am thankful for the times we shared, and I feel blessed to have had a mom that others could only dream of. I have always been and will continue to be proud of my mother for her love of the Lord, her right choices, her ability to lead by example and the contributions she made here on earth. Mom had an unconditional love for all of her children, and as her daughter, I will miss that attribute the most.

We will continue to publish "A Lady's Day Out" books and see her vision through. A percentage of all book sales will go to charity in Mom's memory. Thank you for celebrating her memory with us. Each time you pick up this book or any of our others, we hope you think of Mom and her inspiration—Jesus Christ.

Jennifer "Jenni" Ramsey

The Rusty Bucket

The Rusty Bucket
(See related story page 113.)

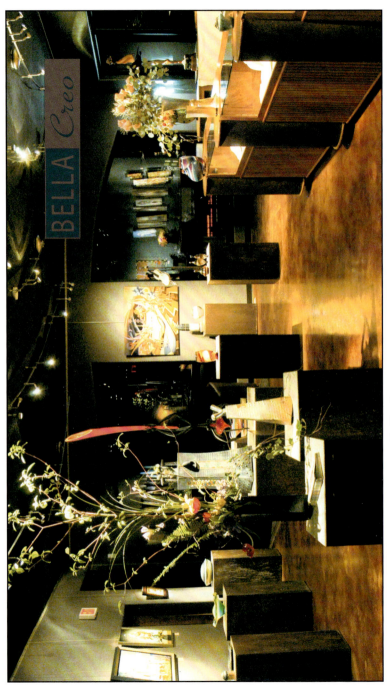

Bella Creo *(See related story page 103.)*

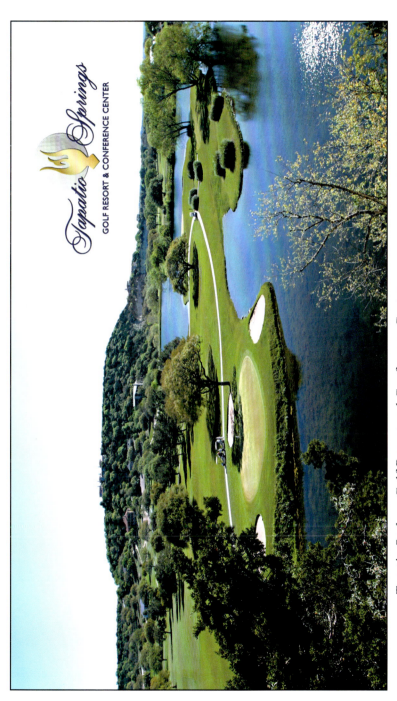

Tapatio Springs Golf Resort and Conference Center *(See related stories page 108 and 120.)*

The Jackson House

The Ogé House

Aaron Pancoast Carriage House

Noble Inns *(See related story page 42.)*

Photo credit: Jumping Rocks

Sattler Artisans' Alley *(See related story page 133.)*

Hideout on the Horseshoe *(See related story page 146.)*

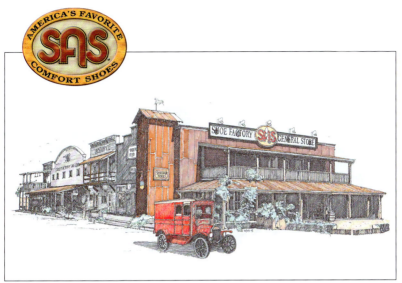

SAS Shoe Factory and General Store
(See related story page 38.)

Catrina's at the Ranch
(See related story page 115.)

IX

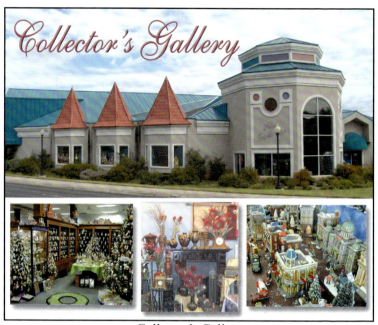

Collector's Gallery
(See related story page 62.)

Alamo City's Little Flower Inn
(See related story page 40.)

The Green Bull Jewelry Co. *(See related story page 118.)*

The Gallery
of Ligthing
(See related story page 115.)

Drums' Lakeview Resort *(See related stories page 136 and 147.)*

XII

STRAWMANOR

Strawmanor is a gracious Hill Country resort with a beautiful and special history. Greg and Bernardine Tomko began building their "straw house" in Canyon Lake, but before they could finish it Greg passed away. Herb Nordmeyer, an expert in construction materials, used his connections with the Straw Bale Association of Texas to recruit volunteers to complete the dream Bernardine's husband had started. Straw Manor, 417 Simon Crest, is available for family reunions, business retreats, intimate weddings and special events for as many as 75 people. The four large bedrooms comfortably sleep 16 adults. The 600-square-foot restaurant-style kitchen is perfect for entertaining, and the handsome great room features built in speakers for music or presentations. Step outside onto the gazebo and commune with nature and wildlife, and enjoy the incredible beauty of the Texas Hill Country. Visit www.strawmanor.com to see the warm interior, the inviting exterior and the breathtaking views of Strawmanor. Call 866-860-4007 for reservations or information.

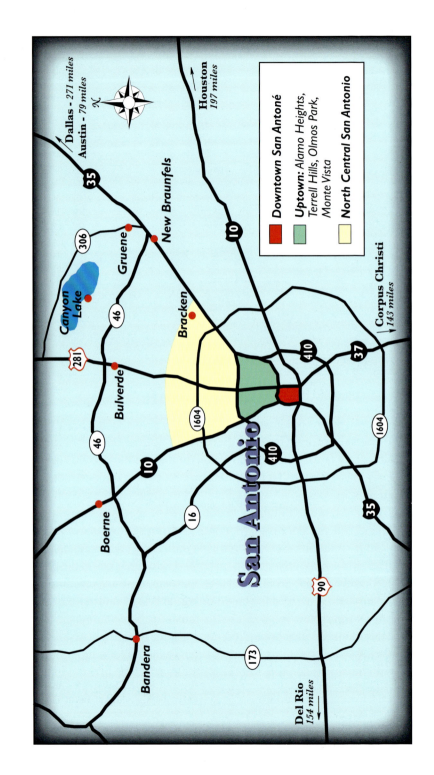

Available Titles

After enjoying this book, we are sure you will also love our other books:

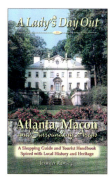

"A LADY'S DAY OUT IN ATLANTA, MACON AND SURROUNDING AREAS"
The breathtaking beauty of the North Georgia Mountains, the sophistication of Atlanta and the rich history of the Historic Heartland region are all featured in this must-have shopping guide and tourist handbook. Visitors and locals alike will enjoy the delightful stories that guide you to the best shopping, lodging, dining and luxury services, as well as exciting attractions and entertainment. This book is the perfect companion when visiting Atlanta and Macon, as well as Athens, Blue Ridge, Bolingbroke, Buckhead, Canton, Cave Spring, Cleveland, Covington, Dahlonega, Dawsonville, Decatur, Helen, Juliette, Madison, Marietta, Milledgeville, Newnan, Old Town Sharpsburg, Perry, Pine Mountain, Rome, Roswell, Sautee Nacoochee, Smyrna, Social Circle, Stone Mountain, Warm Springs, Warner Robins, Watkinsville and Woodstock.
Hard Cover — *325 Pages - $19.95*

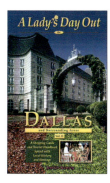

"A LADY'S DAY OUT IN DALLAS AND SURROUNDING AREAS"
From the glitz and glamour of Dallas to the Historic Square of Gainesville, we found the most delightful shopping, scrumptious dinning, luxurious bed & breakfasts and inns and so much more! Let us guide you through the Big "D" and 20 charming surrounding towns and cities. This book is a must for visitors and "Dallas Natives" alike. Featuring Dallas and the enchanting towns of Allen, Carrollton, Cedar Hill, Coppell, DeSoto, Duncanville, Flower Mound, Forney, Frisco, Gainesville, Garland, Irving, Lancaster, Lewisville, McKinney, Plano, Richardson, Rockwall, Sherman & Waxahachie. Hard Cover — *270 Pages - $19.95*

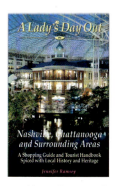

"A LADY'S DAY OUT IN NASHVILLE, CHATTANOOGA AND SURROUNDING AREAS"
From the rolling hills and mountains to Music City USA or the world's largest freshwater aquarium, Tennessee has got it going on! Discover Tennessee like you've never experienced it, with the help of our 19th book. "A Lady's Day Out in Nashville, Chattanooga and Surrounding Areas." You'll find the best shopping, lodging, eating and pampering services that each town has to offer, while learning the area's history, its special attractions, its extraordinary people and its calendar of events. This book is a must-have for those planning a getaway to: Nashville, Chattanooga, Bell Buckle, Brentwood, Clarksville, Clifton, Cookeville, Crossville, Dickson, Fayetteville, Franklin, Gallatin, Goodlettsville, Hendersonville, Lawrenceburg, Lebanon, Leipers Fork, Lynchburg, Murfreesboro, Pickwick, Savannah, Shelbyville, Signal Mountain and Waynesboro.
Hard Cover — *280 Pages - $19.95*

"A LADY'S DAY OUT ON NORTHWEST FLORIDA'S EMERALD COAST"

Sparkling, emerald green waters along miles of pristine sugar white sand beaches make the Emerald Coast breathtaking! You'll find beachside restaurants, shopping treasures, relaxing accommodations and sun-kissed attractions among the unhurried world along the Gulf. This book is the perfect companion guide to adventurers exploring the warmth and hospitality of Apalachicola, Carillon Beach, Destin, Fort Walton Beach, Grayton Beach, Gulf Breeze, Mexico Beach, Navarre Beach, Niceville, Pace, Panama City Beach, Pensacola, Pensacola Beach, Port St. Joe, Rosemary Beach, Sandestin, Santa Rosa Beach, Seagrove Beach, Seaside, Shalimar and Valparaiso. — *237 Pages - $19.95*

"A LADY'S DAY OUT IN THE TEXAS HILL COUNTRY, VOLUME II"

Spiced with local history and heritage; this book is our latest edition for the Texas Hill Country. Featuring the best bed & breakfasts, inns, cottages, art galleries, antiques, tearooms, restaurants, unique boutiques, specialty shops, attractions and entertainment the Hill Country has to offer. Find out why the Texas Hill Country is a favorite destination for all. Plan your trip by using this book and you'll be sure to guide yourself to the best and most unique towns and shops the Hill Country has to offer. Featuring the wonderful towns of Bandera, Boerne, Medina, Vanderpool, Blanco, Brady, Brownwood, Early, Burnet, Buchanan Dam, Comfort, Fredericksburg, Goldwaite, Hamilton, Johnson City, Stonewall, Junction, Kerrville, Ingram, Lampasas, Llano, Marble Falls, Kingsland, Mason and Wimberley. — *250 Pages - $18.95*

"A LADY'S DAY OUT IN MISSISSIPPI"

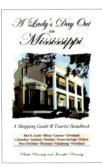

Southern charm and uniqueness drip from the pages of this Shopping Guide and Tourist Handbook. We have found true Mississippi treasures! As always great shopping, dining and lodging fill the pages of this book in this fascinating state. Bay St. Louis, Biloxi, Canton, Cleveland, Columbus, Jackson, Natchez, Ocean Springs, Oxford, Pass Christian, Picayune, Vicksburg and Waveland are all covered. — *212 Pages - $17.95*

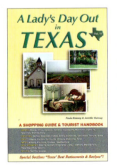

"A LADY'S DAY OUT IN TEXAS, VOL. III"

Features 37 new "GET-A-WAY" Texas towns—most are new and not covered in Texas, Vol. II—brimming with fascinating history and delightful, unique shopping. Inside you'll find all the details about romantic bed & breakfasts and inns, fabulous antique shops, lovely art galleries, home décor, gift shops and exciting entertainment, tearooms, soda fountains and much more. — *276 Pages - $18.95*

— **BOOKS SOON TO BE AVAILABLE** —
"A Lady's Day Out in the Texas Hill Country, Vol. III"

Book Order Form

A Lady's Day Out, Inc.
8551 Boat Club Road #117 • Fort Worth, Tx 76179
Toll Free: 1-888-860-ALDO (2536)

Please send _____ copies of "**A LADY'S DAY OUT IN SAN ANTONIO & SURROUNDING AREAS, VOL. II**" at $19.95 per copy, plus $4.00 S/H for each book ordered. (Tax included.)

Please send _____ copies of "**A LADY'S DAY OUT IN ATLANTA, MACON & SURROUNDING AREAS**" at $19.95 per copy, plus $4.00 S/H for each book ordered. (Tax included.)

Please send _____ copies of "**A LADY'S DAY OUT IN DALLAS & SURROUNDING AREAS, VOL. II**" at $19.95 per copy, plus $4.00 S/H for each book ordered. (Tax included.)

Please send _____ copies of "**A LADY'S DAY OUT IN NASHVILLE, CHATTANOOGA & SURROUNDING AREAS**" at $19.95 per copy, plus $4.00 S/H for each book ordered. (Tax included.)

Please send _____ copies of "**A LADY'S DAY OUT ON NORTHWEST FLORIDA'S EMERALD COAST**" at $19.95 per copy, plus $4.00 S/H for each book ordered. (Tax included.)

Please send _____ copies of "**A LADY'S DAY OUT IN THE TEXAS HILL COUNTRY, VOL. II**" at $18.95 per copy, plus $4.00 S/H for each book ordered. (Tax included.)

Please send _____ copies of "**A LADY'S DAY OUT IN MISSISSIPPI**" at $17.95 per copy, plus $4.00 S/H for each book ordered. (Tax included.)

Please send _____ copies of "**A LADY'S DAY OUT IN TEXAS VOL. III**" at $18.95 per copy, plus $4.00 S/H for each book ordered. (Tax included.)

Please send _____ copies of "**A LADY'S DAY OUT IN THE RIO GRANDE VALLEY & SOUTH PADRE ISLAND**" at $17.95 per copy, plus $4.00 S/H for each book ordered. (Tax included.)

Please send _____ copies of "**A KID'S DAY OUT IN THE DALLAS/FORT WORTH METROPLEX, VOL. I**" at $16.95 per copy, plus $4.00 S/H for each book ordered. (Tax included.)

MAIL BOOKS TO:

NAME: _____

ADDRESS: _____

CITY_____ STATE_____ ZIP_____

AMOUNT ENCLOSED: _____

CREDIT CARD ORDERS CALL: 1-888-860-ALDO (2536)

www.aladysdayout.com

A Lady's Day Out

IN

San Antonio
& Surrounding Areas

VOLUME II

A Shopping Guide & Tourist Handbook

— featuring —

Alamo Heights • Bandera • Boerne • Bracken
Bulverde • Canyon Lake • Gruene • Monte Vista
New Braunfels • Olmos Park • Terrell Hills

by Jennifer Ramsey

Cover features The Ogé House
(See related story on page 42.)

CREDITS

Editor/Author
Jennifer Ramsey

Director of Research & Sales
Jennifer Ramsey

Administrative & Production
Kay Payne
Laura Pender

Editor & Writer
Gena Maselli

Research & Sales
Margaret Neilson
David McBride

Contributing Writers
Jenny Harper Nahoum
Gena Maselli
Barbie Jenkins

Lanette Pannell
Thalia Heistand
Jeanne Anderson

Copyright 2007
A Lady's Day Out, Inc.
ISBN 13: 978-1-891527-18-0
ISBN 10: 1-891527-18-5

Paid advertising by invitation only.

Produced by
A Lady's Day Out, Inc.

Printed in the United States of America
by Armstrong Printing Company, Austin, Texas

Table of Contents

Note from the Author .... *iv*

Bienvenidos Amigos a la San Antonio *1*

Shining Stars of San Antonio—Its People *9*

Discover Downtown San Antoné & Uptown Loop *21*
   (Alamo Heights, Terrell Hills, Olmos Park and
   Monte Vista)

Discover North Central San Antonio / *53*
   Bulverde / Bracken

Discover Bandera *76*

Discover Boerne *95*

Discover New Braunfels / Gruene / Canyon Lake *122*

Index *179*

Cross Reference *182*

Note from the Author

A Lady's Day Out has ventured out on yet another quest to introduce our readers to as many wonderful and fantastic destinations as possible. This time, our travels led us to San Antonio, and I have Good News for everyone—the city of San Antonio is as enchanting and charming as ever. With this chunk of Texas real estate's recent growth explosion, concerns arose that the qualities we once found so endearing might have been lost. Thankfully, we were wrong! The city's warmth and graciousness, uncanny ability to find any reason to celebrate, and open arms to all visitors, are still part of her endearing signature. So pack your bags and make a beeline to this amazing city. All the "wonderful" of the past is now complemented by the "exciting" of the new. It's like the cherry on top of a very delicious sundae! That's right, San Antonio has grown and improved without losing any of the qualities that made her so special. Kudos, San Antonio, for a job well done!

As we continued on our journey, we landed in Bandera, Boerne, New Braunfels, Gruene and Canyon Lake. These delightful towns drip with interesting history, intoxicating local flavor and matchless charm, all served up in true Texas style. Each has such distinct character, bringing something different to the table and making them what I like to refer to as "destination worthy." It's a title I have proudly bestowed on towns that offer a plethora of shopping, dining, lodging and, above all, great fun.

Whether you are new to San Antonio, a longtime native, or simply a visitor, use this book to guide you through this one-of-a-kind city and the captivating, surrounding Hill Country towns. *A Lady's Day Out* has explored and investigated each of these places for you. Have fun, buy lots of treasures and be sure to let us know how your adventure turns out.

Jenni

Bienvenidos Amigos a la San Antonio

Welcome friends—to San Antonio, a vibrant, spirited city rich in culture, history, art, adventure and fun! There is an undeniable magic in San Antonio and the beautiful surrounding Hill Country. You'll find it in the lush history of its famous Riverwalk, in the easy blend of its many cultures, in the spirited festivals that draw visitors from around the world, and in its historical tributes. Each year, millions of visitors enjoy the delights and charm of San Antonio— her romance and adventure, Mexican and German heritage and outstanding recreational opportunities.

Where else could you explore colonial plazas that date from 1731, see a floating parade, sip a margarita at an open-air café, visit a wax museum, be splashed by a killer whale and see the famous "Alamo?" San Antonio is *so* much fun! The city is quiet and serene in some areas and hopping with excitement in others. It is a picture perfect getaway—a Mexican serenade on a starlit night, a romantic sunset cruise on the river, a heaping plate of sizzling fajitas and new friends who open their city to visitors with warm smiles and spicy food. San Antonio will swirl and twirl its way into your heart as fast as you say "Mariachi" and you will remember the sun-kissed moments of her charms for a lifetime.

In the words of a country western song by the Texas band Emory Quinn, "Don't it make you smile, dancin' on Saltillo tile, underneath the stars in downtown San Antone?" San Antonio does make you smile, and dance, and feast and wonder and . . . remember. In one weekend you can visit The Alamo, follow the Mission Trail, hop on a trolley to La Villita, shop at Market Square, explore the tropical Riverwalk and dance beneath the stars on Mexican Saltillo tile! With a few more days to enjoy you can thrill to the rides, shows and water fun at either Fiesta Texas or Sea World, spend time with the wild animals at the San Antonio Zoo, or tour the mansions in the King William Historical District. End your evenings with a horse-drawn carriage ride through town and experience the romance and wonder of the city at night.

Out and About

A short drive into the breathtaking Hill Country leads you into the charming towns of **Boerne** and **New Braunfels**—incredible beauty, fields of striking wildflowers, abundant wildlife, and a delicious slice of German culture. Here you will see the evidence of early German settlers in the historic *fachwerk* houses with gingerbread trim, and enjoy German food and beer in delightful *Bier Gartens*. The beautiful community of **Canyon Lake** offers water lovers miles and miles of tubing fun on the Guadalupe and Comal Rivers, delightful sailing and water skiing adventures on Canyon Lake and even "dinosaur discovery." These day trips add a delicious and memorable addition to your visit to San Antonio, the "Yellow Rose of Texas!"

San Antonio has so much to offer visitors, and one of her most endearing attributes is the warmth and kindness of her people. Although it is a large, sophisticated city, it is casual and informal, and visitors feel welcome, safe and comfortable as they explore downtown, the Riverwalk and the interesting neighborhoods. Its ethnic diversity and blend of cultures make the city a fascinating combination of color and character.

Los Pobladores – The Settlers

Long before the first Spaniards found their way to what is now San Antonio in 1691, Native Americans occupied the land. When a band of Spanish explorers and missionaries happened upon the area along the springs, they named the river San Antonio because it was the feast day of St. Anthony. The official founding in 1718 by Father Antonio Olivares established Mission San Antonio de Valero, which later became known as The Alamo. San Antonio remained under Spanish rule for 103 years until 1821 when Mexico won its independence. Texas became a state and entered the union in 1846 after fighting and winning freedom from Mexico in 1836.

San Antonio's first settlers, (pobladores primeros) were 16 families of Canary Islanders plus a few Tlasca Indians from Mexico. Many descendants of these Canary Islanders remain in San Antonio today. After the Civil War, San Antonio became a true "cow town," with cowboys, cattlemen and cattle drives. During the cattle trail drives, the Chisholm Trail (from the Rio Grande to Kansas) ran right through the city.

When Fort Sam Houston was built in 1876, San Antonio also became known as a "military town." Today, it is one of the nation's top military centers. President Theodore Roosevelt even trained his Rough Riders here! The military has always played a huge part in the city's history and character, especially during World War II. In fact, the area has four active military bases, including Fort Sam Houston, Brooks Air Force Base, Lackland Air Force Base and Randolph Air Force Base.

Though San Antonio's Mexican heritage is very prevalent, many cultures played important roles in the city's early history. It is a melting pot of cultures, including Spanish, Native American, Anglo, German, African American, Polish and Lebanese. During the mid 1800s German immigrants found their way to Texas, and especially to the Hill Country areas of Boerne and New Braunfels and San Antonio. Most of these German pioneers settled in the area known today as the King William Historical District, and many famous businesses and historic homes bear the names of those early German pioneers. One of the earliest Germans to settle San Antonio was Carl Guenther, who built Pioneer Flour Mill on the banks of the river, and the historic Guenther House is open for tours. The prestigious Menger Hotel was built by German immigrant Mr. William Menger in 1859, and a visit to King William would not be complete without a tour of the magnificent Steves Homestead, which was built in 1876.

San Antonio has always had an international flavor, helped perhaps, by the large number of world-traveling service men stationed at the many military bases in the area. Bringing to life the story of the many cultures that make up the face of San Antonio is the **Institute of Texan Cultures**, which depicts the city's early history, and contributions by almost every ethnic group that settled here. You'll see spinning wheels and looms, tools and cooking utensils, an authentic Western chuck wagon, pioneer clothing, early types of transportation, and history documented with incredible photos and letters. One of the best times to visit the Institute is during the summer for the Texas Folklife Festival.

San Antonio Today

The face of San Antonio today is as diverse as the colors of the confetti in a cascarone. It is a college town, an art scene, a queen of festivals, a shopping Mecca, a famous historical destination, and home to The San Antonio Spurs, a world champion NBA basketball team (four trophies!). San Antonio has grown through the years from a small mission town to an important military location, to a city recognized as an industry leader, and top tourist destination. It is a mixture of the preserved past and always changing future. San Antonio's population has exploded from 3,500 people in 1836 (the year Texas won independence from Mexico) to near 1.6 million today. It is indeed a center for culture diversity, with almost 60 percent of the population being Latino.

Although "College Town" might not be the first word that comes to mind when you hear the name San Antonio, there are five major universities and many community colleges located here. The University of Texas at San Antonio registers more than 28,000 students each year, and the University of the Incarnate Word attracts students from many countries. Other public and private San Antonio colleges include Trinity University, Our Lady of the Lake University, St. Mary's University, and community colleges that include San Antonio College, St. Phillip's College, Palo Alto College and Northwest Vista College.

San Antonio's "art scene" is growing and evolving each year, with new galleries opening and up-and-coming San Antonio artists being recognized throughout the nation. A must-visit on your trip to San Antonio is the **McNay Art Museum**, the state's oldest private modern art museum, which is housed in the mansion of its founder, Marion Koogler McNay. The **San Antonio Museum of Art** is well known for its collections of antiquities—Mexican folk art, pre-Columbian, Spanish, colonial and modern art. The **Witte Museum**, on Broadway, also features constantly changing exhibits for all ages. Other top museums include the **San Antonio Children's**

Museum, the **Blue Star Contemporary Art Center**, **ArtPace**, and the **Museo Alameda** (a Smithsonian affiliate) in Market Square, which is devoted to the Latino experience in America.

If "lions and tigers and bears" are more your idea of fun, the **San Antonio Zoo** promises a "Real WILD Life" experience. The Zoo had its start in 1914, when Colonel George W. Brackenridge, one of the city's leading citizens gathered a few buffalo, deer, monkeys, elk, lions and bears on land he had deeded to the city. The small collection of animals has grown through the years to house more than 3,800 animals representing more than 750 species. The Zoo is extremely excited about the new project called, "Africa Live!" which will take visitors on an expedition through the Dark Continent.

And, of course we could not talk about the excitement of San Antonio without mentioning her beloved San Antonio Spurs. The city is passionate about their Spurs—four-time National Championship winners. During the games, downtown is filled with decorated trucks and cars, silver and black clad fans of all ages, confetti, horns and lots of excitement.

From rodeos with billboard musicians in February and the glory of Fiesta in April to the Texas Folklife Festival in June, Fall Art Festivals and the Texas Open in October, San Antonio celebrates throughout the entire year. This exuberant spirit of celebration and fun is one of the city's most endearing characteristics you will experience any time you visit.

Viva Fiesta!

Long Live the Party! San Antonio celebrates in grand style during the spring when "Fiesta" takes over the entire city. In fact, for ten days every April, the entire city is one big party. Fiesta always takes place during the week of San Jacinto Day, and celebrates Texas' independence from Mexico. Ethnic celebrations, parades, fancy balls, carnivals, and art and music festivals fill every minute of every day with the spirit of Fiesta.

Four main parades sell out every year. The Texas Cavaliers River Parade takes place on the first Monday evening of Fiesta. It is a glorious presentation of more than 50 floats down the San Antonio River. The Battle of Flowers Parade, held on Friday, is the largest and oldest Fiesta parade. It is so popular that most schools proclaim

"Battle of Flowers" day a standard holiday. This day parade had its beginnings in 1891 with carriages decorated with flowers and floats drawn by horses. When the carriages ended at The Alamo, the ladies inside began throwing flowers at each other, thus the name "Battle of Flowers Parade." The third and most elaborate parade is called the Fiesta Flambeau, and is held on the following Saturday night. Young and old camp out for spots to see this parade. All of the floats are lit up and even the marching bands and entertainers carry flashlights. Last, but not least, the King William Fair offers a more relaxed atmosphere for family fun. This street parade is a favorite every year.

Fiesta always includes honorary royalty of two kings, King Antonio and El Ray Feo, many queens, and duchesses in fancy gowns. These royal figures rule the city with one goal—to spread good cheer and fun! During four nights of Fiesta the downtown area of La Villita turns into a street party called NIOSA (Night in Old San Antonio) complete with food, drink and entertainment booths from many cultures. The streets are lined with booths selling scrumptious delicacies like German sausage on a stick, Black Forest cake, empanadas, antichuchos, gorditas fried oysters and escargot. Oh, and there's plenty of beer and margaritas!

From oyster bakes and oompah celebrations to dog shows and masked balls, there is something for everyone during Fiesta. However, one of the most elaborate events takes place on Wednesday night—the crowning of the Order of the Alamo Queen. Here, debutantes are presented in magnificent gowns covered in thousands of beads and jewels, and these same duchesses are one of the main attractions on the Battle of Flowers and Flambeau parades.

On the flip side of this traditional grandeur, the "Cornyation" is a romp-roaring, slightly risqué presentation that mocks the Coronation and addresses just about every political issue in the city. As you can see, a visit to San Antonio during Fiesta will definitely be an experience you will remember!

Remember The Alamo!

It's the first thing guests want to see when visiting San Antonio. And, they are always a little surprised that it is right in the middle of downtown. Mission San Antonio de Valero—The Alamo—is of course San Antonio's most famous and treasured attraction. In fact, it is the #1 tourist attraction in all of Texas! The story of The Alamo and its defenders has been told time and time again, in history books and through television and cinema. Davy Crockett, Jim Bowie, William Travis and 186 others are larger-than-life heroes who protected The Alamo in a fight for Texas' freedom and died within the walls of the historic mission.

It was established in 1718 as the city's first mission, and the chapel is one of the most photographed facades in the country. The Mission was renamed The Alamo (a Spanish word for cottonwood), because beautiful cottonwood trees surrounded the structure. The long barracks museum and library have been restored near the old chapel with pictures and relics recalling Texas' War for Independence from Mexico.

The Battle of The Alamo changed not only the face of San Antonio, but was also a turning point in the history of Texas and the entire Southwest. On February 23, 1836, Mexican General Antonio Lopez de Santa Anna marched into San Antonio with more than 4,000 troops and raised a red banner at San Fernando Cathedral indicating there would be no quarter (no surrender). William B. Travis answered with a cannon shot, and the Battle of The Alamo began. Travis' famous letter that asked for help was answered by only 32 young men from Gonzales, and for 13 days the 189 defenders held The Alamo against continuous siege by Santa Anna. On March 6, the 13th day of the battle, Colonel Travis drew the "line in the sand," asking that all who would stand with him for Texas cross the line. Jim Bowie, who was wounded, asked that his cot be carried across that line. At 5:00 a.m., March 6, 1836, the Mexican bugler sounded "Deguello," and the troops charged The Alamo. The Battle of The Alamo ended at 6:30 a.m. Historians believe that although The Alamo fell, this battle enabled the Texas army to defeat the weakened Mexican troops in San Jacinto, securing the state's independence from Mexico.

The Mission Trail

After The Alamo was built (1718), four more missions were established along the San Antonio River during the early and mid 1700s. Their purpose was to convert the local Native Americans into Catholics and serve as educational centers. All five of these historical missions are still standing, some with extensive renovation. All are open to the public for tours and some for church services. Besides The Alamo, the remaining four missions make up what is called the **San Antonio Missions National Historical Park**, and some still operate as Catholic churches.

You can retrace the path of the early missionaries in one day (or even a half day) beginning at Mission Road, just north of Hwy. 90, but it is too large an area to cover on foot.

Mission Concepcion, 807 Mission Rd. (1731) – One of the oldest un-restored stone churches in the country. All that remains of the mission is a handsome twin-towered church with two bell towers.

Mission San Jose, 6701 San Jose Dr. (1720) – The largest of the missions. Visitors can still see the choir loft and the 25 risers that were hand-hewn from a single log without nails or pegs.

Mission San Juan Capistrano, 9101 Graf Rd. – This mission was moved to San Antonio from East Texas and was a thriving agricultural center. The farmers who lived around the mission were so successful that they provided produce to the other mission areas. Daily mass is still held in this historical mission.

Mission San Francisco De La Espada, 10040 Espada Rd., (1731) – The smallest and most isolated of the five San Antonio missions. It also was moved to San Antonio from East Texas.

There is a famous Texas historian and journalist by the name of Frank Tolbert that described San Antonio to a "T." He said, "Every Texan has two homes, his own and San Antonio." So true. We think that after your visit here you will want to make San Antonio *your* second home. Our research for this book was so much fun! We hope you will enjoy learning about all of the wonderful and charming places we found to stay, dine, shop and explore in The Alamo city. Your experience will be one of color, music, dance, excitement and fun, and the Tex-Mex locals of San Antonio will role out the "yellow" carpet in true South Texas style. Bienvenidos!

Shining Stars of San Antonio – Its People

DON YARTON

His client list reads like a "Who's Who" in San Antonio. During the last 40 years he has furnished and decorated houses from coast to coast. His fine antiques have been photographed and featured in *Veranda, Southern Living* and *Vogue*, and his name is synonymous with excellence and style. Don Yarton is today a San Antonio icon in the world of art and antiques—a true San Antonio star.

With his piercing steel blue "Paul Newman" eyes, striking white hair and easy smile, Don is charming and sophisticated, a man perfectly at ease with his life and career. Known throughout San Antonio and the United States as an expert in the world of antiques and art, Don continues to live up to his reputation for having a keen eye for beauty, authenticity and value. His travels throughout the country and abroad afford him the opportunity to find exquisite treasures from around the world.

After a stint in the army as a youth, Don began his civilian life with a grand total of $800 in his pocket and a big dream to "make a lot of money in the antique business." He laughs today at that naïve young man who thought that buying and selling antiques would be an easy way to make a living.

"It was a *hard* way to make a small living then," he says. "In fact, I think you have to have a head full of white hair before anyone really takes you seriously in this business."

Don persevered through the years, always studying, always learning and always discovering more of what he loved about antiques. He began to collect one-of-a-kind antiques, creating showrooms filled with unique and valuable pieces of art. Today, he is known as one of the most knowledgeable authorities in the country of 17th, 18th and 19th century antiques, and is considered the most prestigious name in the San Antonio antique industry.

In the recent move from a long time downtown location, Don Yarton Antiques and Accessories is now located in one of San Antonio's most recognizable landmarks—the Mobil building at the corner of Broadway and Austin Hwy. The antique Pegasus that tops the building has been distinguished as a historical marker and belongs to the San Antonio Conservation Society. Don's outstanding collection of antiques seems perfectly at home in this setting. Through the years the building has housed many different businesses, but seems now to have found its perfect partner in Don Yarton Antiques and Accessories.

It is definitely a unique space. No "granny" antiques or small collectibles here. Don's collection of period pieces from the 17th, 18th and 19th century are impressive in both size and content. In fact, one could easily imagine the characters from Don's all-time favorite movie, "Dangerous Liaisons," settling within these rooms of beautiful tapestry and art.

Giant rustic red barn doors flank the entrance, and an 18th century day bed canopied in Aubergine toile takes center stage. (There is even an identical canopied doggie bed!) Throughout the space, beautiful bronzes rest atop massive pillars, and carved painted "Santos" bless the room. Inlaid wood tables and enameled trays hold candelabras and exquisite porcelains, and intricate 17th century French and Flemish tapestries cover the stucco walls. There are 18th century cabinets that hold blue and white collections and Cuban chests that work as end tables. Framed original oil paintings grace the walls and beautiful chandeliers light the rooms. Every item is a piece of art; every piece of art a masterpiece.

What inspired Don to create such memorable settings with antiques and art? "Museum collections, compendiums of furniture, beautiful photographs—I fell in love with photographs and fine art and studied constantly," he says. "By traveling I began to realize that these magnificent pieces of high-end art and furniture were still accessible; that they were not prohibitive." He says that he was also influenced by the internationally recognized artists that make up Lloyd-Paxton, of Dallas. Their work has continued to inspire me through the years."

As I sat with him for this interview, several customers came in to browse. His easy going, friendly manner set them at ease in this room filled with such breathtaking grandeur. In fact, one young woman came in search of a desk, and by the end of her visit had purchased several other items and learned that Don knew her entire family. Don's name is one that has traveled through the years with generations of San Antonians as they moved from home to home. His pieces have decorated sprawling West Texas ranch homes and elegant King William, Terrell Hills and Monte Vista mansions. One of the things that his customers have appreciated the most is that he is extremely knowledgeable about his antiques and so eager to share it with others.

Don says, "People love learning the history behind each piece, what makes it so special, and how it will fit so beautifully into their homes and lives."

In fact, teaching is something that Don wants to pursue. He would love to be able to teach a college class on period antiques. Both customers and other antique dealers come to him for advice and mentoring, and he is always honored to help.

The excellent advice he gave one young woman (and me as I took notes) was this, "Buy two great pieces every year. Really stretch to purchase two items, even if it's a little painful. If it sings to your heart, buy it. It will make you happy. Every time you walk by it you will know, 'I love this.' In a few years you will have a wonderful collection of quality antiques, and your other furnishings will find their place around these pieces."

Don Yarton is one of the most interesting men you will meet during your visit to San Antonio. He is a respected patron to the antique and art world who has created a legacy of beauty and history within the walls of his remarkable showroom. I'm going to take his advice! *(See related story on page 30.)*

SHINING STARS OF SAN ANTONIO — ITS PEOPLE **11**

VIOLA MECKEL &
MARGIE MECKEL SKOLAUT

"A River Runs Through It!"

Just off IH-35 and Loop 337 you will come to one of the prettiest places in the New Braunfels area—River Road. This winding country road turns through beautiful shaded country that fronts the Guadalupe River. The river flows right beside you as you meander through miles and miles of quiet beauty that literally takes your breath away. As you cross the river once, then twice and then three times you'll see rentals, cabins on stilts, ice houses, river outfitters, picnic tables and lots of tents and RV campers. After the third crossing you'll come to one of the oldest river outfitters and campgrounds in the area the Lazy L & L Campgrounds—and meet an incredible German family who has spent a lifetime working the land and promoting the beauty of the Guadalupe River. The Lazy L & L has been a home-away-from-home for thousands of weekend campers and Winter Texans for decades, and now, new generations are returning to float, tube, canoe or kayak, and enjoy the beauty of this land that "the river runs through."

Margie and Rodney Skolaut now manage the business that was started during the early 1970s by her parents Louis and Viola Meckel. The Lazy L & L is located on acres of absolutely beautiful country with wonderful river frontage.

Viola Meckel, now 94, is still an elegant and lovely woman whose joy in life is seeing the fruition of their hard work in the successful business, in the happiness of her children and grandchildren, and in her many friends. Of course, the old German card game "SKAT" has been known to bring a smile to her face too!

The Lazy L & L is located on land that has been in the Meckel family for generations. Viola Preusser's family owned lots of the farmland surrounding the Meckels. She and Louis grew up during the early 1900s working the land with their families. As children both Viola and Louis attended Mountain Valley School in Sattler. Within this large German community their lives consisted of lots of "hard work" and a little "hard play."

"We worked from sunup to sunset," says Viola, "Thrashing oats, picking cotton, baling hay—working every minute of every day." When they did take time to "play" Viola remembers wonderful community birthday bashes and exciting dances in New Braunfels at Landa Park. She says that folks would come from all around the county to the dances, and that the musicians would perform from platforms built up in the trees. The Comal County Fair was an annual event then that is still going strong today. "We looked forward to the fair all year—we got a new 'dress,' not jeans and boots like today," says Viola.

Viola Preusser and Louis Meckel married in 1933 and lived in a small room on the Meckel land. There was no electricity, no running water and no heat. They worked side by side every day, living almost entirely "off the land."

Viola says, "We grew everything we needed—all of our vegetables and fruit, and what we didn't eat we canned or put up for the winter months. We had cows for meat and milk and chickens for eggs. We lived very simply, but had everything we needed!"

Times were hard in the rugged country. Viola remembers the time even before outhouses. Even after they got their outhouse, "paper" was hard to come by. She laughs and says, "My sister married a man a little better off than we were, and they actually had a Sears catalog in the outhouse—that was rich!"

The Meckels were married for 18 years before the birth of their daughter Margie.

"She was the community miracle baby," Viola says. "Everyone had prayed for her birth for such a long time, and we were so surprised when it happened." Sattler area was such a tightly woven community of old German families and friends that they all thought of Margie as one of their own.

Margie grew up on the farmland and worked hard alongside her parents doing everything from helping with the crops to rounding up cattle from the pastures.

"I remember coming in from the pasture and having to take all of my clothes off outside because of "sea ticks," she says. "There would be thousands all over our bodies, and we would have to make sure we got them all. Nature took care of the sea ticks with the arrival of fire ants. Lots of fire ants—no sea ticks!"

Although the beautiful Guadalupe River ran right through their property, no one ever considered it recreation, and especially not the type that would become a business. Margie remembers that as a young child they went fishing with cane poles from time to time, but not very often. Like her parents, she went to school and worked on the farm in all of her spare time. It wasn't until the early 1970s that the Meckel family began to look at the river as a form of economic support. As the community grew and the New Braunfels area became a larger tourist attraction, visitors began finding their way out to the beautiful winding River Road to picnic and swim. When people began asking for permission to camp and float, an idea was born that has grown through the years into one of the largest river outfitters and camping facilities on River Road.

"In the beginning, Daddy would throw a few tubes in the back of the pickup truck, and we would drive down the river to rent them to the campers," Margie remembers. "Then he began stacking little pieces of firewood so that they could have campfires."

The idea took off like wildfire, and soon people came from everywhere to picnic and swim or camp alongside the river. In 1972 the Meckels put up 10 picnic tables along the riverfront, and every year added more and more facilities for campers. The family worked the campground and tube business hard during the summer season, and continued to farm the land the rest of the year.

Viola and Louis Meckel loved the work. They loved meeting new people each season, and seeing second generations of families coming back to float and picnic and enjoy their beautiful part of the river and land.

One of the biggest draws to the Lazy L & L Campgrounds is the part of the river known as the Devil's Playground, and everyone on the property has access to it. Paths wind down to a rock ledge for sunbathing. Tubers can float, get out, walk back up, and start over, or take a shuttle from down stream.

Winter Texans have found their way to the Lazy L & L, and absolutely love being tucked back in the tranquil setting surrounded by the graceful rolling hills. With access to the river, electricity and a country store, they have everything they need for a warm winter under the stars of the beautiful Texas Hill Country.

While Margie was growing up and living on the property, there was a young man named Rodney Skolaut who also grew up in the same area. He was almost like family, more like a brother to Margie, and she says they never thought of "dating." During the early tubing years, Rodney would park a truck and trailer on the Meckel property and sell anything he could think of—T-shirts, caps, sausage on a stick and hamburgers. He was a hard worker and loved the Meckels like family. Both Margie and Rodney married other people, and Margie moved away from New Braunfels. It was during that time that Rodney approached the Meckels about leasing the property and business to manage. The Meckels were getting older and the work harder. They knew Rodney loved it as much as they did. Both Margie and Rodney had divorced, and he was running the business when she moved back to New Braunfels in 1993. Their years of growing up together gave them such a strong connection and after a short while they began to date. Their past was instrumental in bringing them together again for a wonderful future, and they were married in 1994.

Louis Meckel died at the age of 89 in 1998, but Viola Meckel remains an important asset to the Lazy L & L. They both made such huge impacts on the lives of so many who visited their property during the years. Campers from the 70s and 80s remember Mr. Meckel on a tractor, hauling firewood, always working, always talking with the campers. Viola Meckel's sweet personality and hard work ethic enabled her to endure many hardships during her life, and definitely influenced family and friends around her. Now at the age of 94, she is still a strong presence in the community. And, you can't talk to her for very long without finding out about two of her passions—SKAT and deer hunting.

Pronounced "Skot," this old German card game is one that was originally played only by men. "In the early days," Viola says, "women weren't considered to be smart enough to play it, and no one would even teach a woman the game." She says that she only learned to play because her husband loved it so much and needed someone to play it with him. She plays in three to four tournaments each year, and with a twinkle in her eye says, "I even beat the men sometimes, and they don't like it very much!"

Viola Meckel's "can do" spirit and positive approach to everything has allowed her to be extremely active and capable, even at the age of 94. In fact, just a few years ago, at the young age of 88 she shot the biggest buck and won the "Big Buck" contest for all of Comal County. She laughs as she remembers the Paul Harvey radio segment and the live broadcast from London entitled, "Granny Get Your Gun!"

Margie and Rodney Skolaut continue to run the Lazy L & L with the same energy and enthusiasm that the early campers came to love in the Meckel family. It is truly an "all in the family" business. Although she and Rodney have been living in New Braunfels, he has always wanted to build a house on the property. Margie says that more and more now she feels drawn back to the land where she grew up—to the deep green valleys and huge hills, and to the water that flows through so much of the land. Her memories of her early years with her mother and father, the hard work and simple times and the beginnings of her life with her "friend" Rodney, all draw her back to the land.

One day, as she was reading her Bible, Margie opened to Ezekiel 36:28 (NIV) and read, "You will live in the land I gave your forefathers; you will be my people, and I will be your God." Margie and Rodney are now building in a valley next to her mother, they now work side-by-side as her mother and father did long ago, and they are thankful that God did indeed bring them both back together, to live on this beautiful land and continue the legacy started long ago by her parents.

"There is such a peace and serenity here," says Margie. "I think that is what attracts so many visitors. For a short weekend or even a winter, they can relax and enjoy God's beautiful country with family and friends away from the hustle and bustle of their every day lives." *(See related story on page 151.)*

THE BARRIOS FAMLY

When Mama Viola B. Barrios opened her tiny, downtown San Antonio restaurant in 1979, it was with $3,000 and lots of prayer. In fact it has been Mama Viola's profound faith in God that has enabled the entire Barrios family to build a family business that now includes two hugely successful restaurants and an important legacy of service to the community. In a city where Mexican food reigns as Queen of Cuisine, Los Barrios Mexican Continental Cuisine is always on a San Antonian's list of favorite places to eat. The food is incredible—good, home-style Mexican food that Mrs. Barrios says is cooked in the Casero style—"from the home, from years of tradition, pride and heritage, handed down from one generation to the next." In addition to the food, the Barrios family, with warm, genuine Tex-Mex hospitality and appreciation for their customers, draws regulars to their tables to celebrate birthdays, anniversaries, reunions, graduations, good grades, home runs, or just Sunday afternoons. Los Barrios feels like home.

The Barrios story is one of perseverance, determination, love and faith. Viola Barrios and her daughter, Diana Barrios-Trevino, shared their journey with A Lady's Day Out. It inspired us and we're sure it will inspire you too, giving you a glimpse into the character of this remarkable San Antonio family.

Today, Los Barrios includes the main location at 4223 Blanco Rd., and the fabulous new La Hacienda de Los Barrios, at 18747 Redland Rd. Los Barrios was named one of the "100 Best New Restaurants in America" by *Esquire* magazine, and has been featured in segments on the Food Network and with Emeril Lagasse on Good Morning America. In fact, most recently, Iron Chef Bobby Flay of the Food Network showed up at the La Hacienda location with cameras rolling to challenge Diana to a "Puffy Taco Throwdown." Well, let's just say that there was hardly a competition. Mama Viola's traditional homemade masa puffy taco filled with shredded chicken, freshly made guacamole, lettuce and tomato won hands down over Flay's rendition with red cabbage filling and peanut sauce. Come on Mr. Flay, this is San Antonio! Diana was also asked to participate in a "Slam Dunk Skillet Showdown" that took place during the NCAA Basketball Finals. She and five other local chefs teamed with six NCAA coaches in a cook-off that made her the coach and Notre Dame's Coach Mike Brey the chef. When it came to a tic, Diana was forced to shoot baskets at the free throw line against a 6'5" Austin chef and won! The showdown was broadcast on the Food Network March 2005, and the skillet hangs proudly on the restaurant wall!

The success that this family now enjoys would have been hard to imagine more than 25 years ago when Los Barrios first opened. "Los Barrios did not begin as a dream but rather as a last hope," Diana wrote in her family cookbook. She attributes the restaurant's present-day success to her mother's ability to embrace hardship and uncertainty with a strong work ethic, one that affected her generation and that of her children. Although Mrs. Barrios speaks little

English (even relying on Diana to translate during this interview), she shouldered the burden of being a single, Hispanic woman in business with great success. She was, indeed, a visionary.

After the Barrios family lost their dear husband and father, Jose Barrios, in 1975, Viola was faced with the challenge of raising her children alone.

"I had to do something for my children," she explains, "so I prayed and prayed to God, always asking Him to help me. I believed with my whole heart that He would bless my family."

That blessing came in 1979, when Mr. Francisco Rodrigues, known by all as "Paco," convinced Viola to open her own restaurant in a $500-a-month garage in downtown San Antonio.

"There was no parking, no windows, and few tables," Diana says. "The chairs didn't even match. There were only three people working at that time, mama, Paco and my brother Louis. At night, they just closed the garage door and locked up."

Viola knew that with a humble ambience, the food had better be good, and it was!

"Great cooking carries with it a lot of forgiveness!" she says. The downtown business people began standing in line for the delicious Los Barrios home-style Mexican food, and it took every minute of every day and the entire family just to keep up.

When the property owner tripled their rent after six months, Viola made the decision to buy property and move their restaurant to its present location on Blanco Rd. It is located in what was once an old Dairy Queen, and the original front door frame is now in the middle of the dining room, with the address numbers 4223 shining brightly above it. Oversized terra cotta pots filled with greenery now hang from the brick walls that once held up the DQ's arched glass walls. Over the years, the family continued working together to produce great Mexican food, developing a following of loyal customers that still come back today.

One year later, in 1981, *Esquire* magazine did a story on Los Barrios, naming it one of the "100 Best New Restaurants in America." Diana says that the phone began ringing off the wall with customers wanting reservations.

"Reservations!" she laughs. "We didn't even know what that was!"

When asked about the emotion involved in looking back over

her life and the incredible legacy she has built at Los Barrios, Mama Viola gets tears in her eyes.

"There was much sacrifice," she explains. "I sacrificed so much time with my little children. I prayed so hard, asking God [to help me] make the right decisions, and for health of all of my family."

The legacy that Mama Viola began in 1979 continues to grow. After graduating from St. Mary's University, son Louis Barrios began implementing his marketing skills in running the business. The oldest sibling, Teresa Barrios, (who Diana said always had the hardest jobs in the kitchen when they were young) graduated from Trinity University and then from the Scholl College of Podiatric Medicine of Chicago, and is a podiatrist here in San Antonio. Diana graduated from St. Mary's University with a marketing degree in 1985 and then joined the family business full time.

Built upon the foundation that his mother laid years before, Louis' innovations took the restaurant to another level. He was named "Restaurateur of the Year" by the San Antonio Restaurant Association, and "Small Business Leader of the Year" by the Greater San Antonio Chamber of Commerce. With Diana's charismatic and effervescent personality, she has become Los Barrios' media representative, and her husband Roland Trevino became the hands-on operation manager in 1995.

For five years, Diana did a bi-monthly cooking segment for local television station WOAI (formerly KMOL). Then in 1999, the food producer for ABC's Good Morning America called her about appearing with none other than Emeril Lagasse. That event truly pushed Los Barrios into a new level of success.

"I cooked Calabacita con Pollo for Emeril," says Diana, "to an audience of eight million people!"

Soon after that appearance she got a call from Pamela Cannon, editor of Random House Publishing, and within three weeks had a contract for the Los Barrios Family Cookbook. Diana says the book took three years to complete, came out in June 2002, sold out in just two months, and is now in its eighth printing. The cookbook's launch took place in Rockefeller Center in New York, and the producer asked Mrs. Barrios to speak. She first insisted that she was too nervous to speak in English, but practiced her lines over and over.

"However, once she got started," Diana laughs, "she stole the show. She was so wonderful, and her authenticity and sincerity showed through so beautifully."

Even her grandchildren were amazed, never having heard her speak so much English. In fact, Mrs. Barrios rarely speaks English to her grandchildren. She has remained adamant that her children and grandchildren be bilingual and bicultural. That goal has served them well, opening many doors through the years.

Mama Viola continues to be a tremendous draw for the loyal customers of Los Barrios. She is at the restaurant every day, except for three days a year—Easter, Thanksgiving and Christmas—when the restaurant is closed.

"Yes, she is here every day," Diana attests, "but she likes the late shift now. She likes to sleep late, exercise, get dressed and then come in to stay late."

As we talked, Mama Viola stopped at many of Los Barrios' tables to say hi to the customers, give hugs and offer words of encouragement. She is well known, greatly loved and very respected in San Antonio, having received many awards over the years. Yes, she has lived, and continues to live, a truly extraordinary life. In fact, her family recently learned that she has been building cinderblock houses in the poor area of Bustamente, Nuevo Leon, Mexico, where she was born. It's one more reminder of Mama Viola's desire is to give to others some of what God has so generously given to her.

"Every day when I get up," Mama Viola says, "I ask God to put in my path someone who really needs help. Sometimes He brings me many!"

While in San Antonio be sure to visit one of the Los Barrios restaurants and meet this lovely family. Their true San Antonio spirit shines throughout the restaurants. In the colorful décor, the Mariachi music, the laughter and joy of the customers and the delicious food, you will experience a little of the true flavor of the city and meet a family whose hard work, faith in God and love for each other and their community has made them one of San Antonio's true "Shining Stars!"

Discover
Downtown San Antoné
& Uptown Loop
(Alamo Heights, Terrell Hills, Olmos Park and Monte Vista)

Although San Antonio has so many wonderful and exciting places to discover and explore, most of the action, color, spice, music, dance and flavor of the city happens in the unique celebrated downtown. The famous Riverwalk draws millions to the city and the historic neighborhoods and shopping districts provide hours and days of tourist pleasure. If you are staying in one of the many extraordinary hotels or bed and breakfasts along the Riverwalk you can explore at leisure. You will get the chance to experience the quiet and serenity of the early morning Riverwalk and the festive, party atmosphere at night. During the day take time to explore the King William Historical District, the Mexican Market and LaVillita.

From downtown to the 410 Loop, there are several neighborhoods that have managed to retain much of their original historic charm. **Alamo Heights, Terrell Hills, Olmos Park** and **Monte Vista** are upscale, unique neighborhoods that have kept the old-fashioned, family-oriented feel of "community" alive through the years. In fact, many of the same families have lived in the same houses for generations. Children grow up and move away to school, then come home to the old neighborhoods to raise their families. San Antonians call these areas "aristocratic," and "old money" neighborhoods. Although there are many upscale shops and businesses in

DISCOVER DOWNTOWN SAN ANTONÉ & UPTOWN LOOP   **21**

these communities, you'll also find streets of "mom and pop" stores, bakeries, candy shops, antique, resale shops, cafés and restaurants.

DOWNTOWN

The Magical Riverwalk

In the very beginning it was water that attracted the first settlers to San Antonio, and it is that same lush riverbank that makes the city Texas' number one vacation destination. In the few minutes it takes to walk 20 feet down a flight of stairs, San Antonio's "other world" emerges. The Riverwalk (or Paseo del Rio) with its tropical foliage, massive cypress trees and sidewalk cafés meanders for miles. It is a soothing oasis below the busy, bustling downtown. Once called *Yanaquana* (which means "refreshing waters") by the Native Americans, the San Antonio River today stretches for more than two and one-half miles from the Municipal Auditorium on the north to the King William Historical District on the south, with northern expansion planned for the future.

Its cobblestone and flagstone paths wind through the middle of downtown leading visitors through a lively combination of charming European style cafés, restaurants, theaters, ice cream parlors, museums and historical monuments. Along the horseshoe-shaped river, towering trees and willows offer shade and lush gardens outline the water. There is even a romantic little island known as "Marriage Island," which is one of the local favorite places to tie the knot. Step aboard a Yanaguana water taxi and enjoy a leisurely trip down the river while you learn the history behind the century old buildings. Or, plan a candlelight dinner cruise for your party and enjoy wonderful food and drink as you tour the city by river.

The Paseo del Rio is especially enchanting during the holiday season when it is transformed into a magical wonderland of lights, song and dance. The Friday after Thanksgiving each year is the day of "The Lighting of the River," (more than 200,000 lights) complete with Santa on a barge who leads a colorful illuminated river parade. (Make reservations early for this event.) Folklorico and Flamenco dancers, carolers in period dress and costumed parade goers add merriment and local color to the river experience.

More than 2,000 glowing candles in sand-filled bags (Luminaries) symbolize the lighting of the way for the Holy Family in the Fiesta de las Luminarias, which takes place every weekend in December. Strolling carolers entertain visitors during the holidays and the Rivercenter Christmas Pageant, a series of beautifully decorated barges that tell the Christmas story, is presented on weekends. One of the most beautiful and touching productions (and my favorite) during the season is Las Posadas on the River Walk, (the shelters) the reenactment of the search for shelter by Mary and Joseph in Bethlehem. Actors make their way down the river trying to find "room in the inn," for the birth of baby Jesus. They are turned away at every location until they arrive at the nativity scene at the Arneson River Theatre.

The Riverwalk also shines brightly in the spring while Fiesta reigns throughout the city. A river parade attracts hundreds of thousands to see more than 50 river-barge floats, decorated with the theme of the parade. Each barge holds costumed participants and a band, and the merriment and festivities can be heard throughout the downtown area. Each summer weekend music and dance fill the Arneson River Theatre, providing magical starlit entertainment at Fiesta Noche del Rio, another fun Riverwalk adventure for the entire family. While The Alamo remains Texas' top tourist attraction, the beautiful Riverwalk follows as the second most visited attraction in the state.

By the way, if you happen to be visiting during St. Patrick's Day don't be surprised if the river looks a little green! Both wee young ones and old come to the Riverwalk for the annual St. Patrick's Day River Parade and Dyeing 'O the River Green. Colorfully decorated floats travel from La Mansion to the Arneson River Theatre to the tunes of the traditional Irish bagpipes and green beer flows freely at the many restaurants and bars along the way. During this time the San Antonio River is temporarily renamed "The River Shannon."

Historic La Villita

A short walk from the river puts you right in the middle of one of San Antonio's most endearing historic attractions—La Villita. It is often called a "hidden treasure," rich with history in a setting alive with artists and artisans, shops and restaurants. San Antonio's very first "neighborhood" was originally populated by Coahuiltecan

Indians, and then groups of Spanish settlers. This group of primitive huts around the city's first mission—Mission San Antonio de Valero—was also used for Spanish soldiers in Santa Anna's army, and was the site of the cannon line during the famous Battle of The Alamo.

The area was named Puebo de Valero, and then La Villita, or "Little Village." It is located along the south bank of the river, and is today a major attraction in downtown San Antonio—a thriving art community filled with quaint shops and cafés. Beginning in the 1870s, European immigrants from France and Germany began to settle the area, and the original neighborhood's cultural and ethnic mix is reflected in the remaining architectural styles. As the city's population began to grow northward during the early 1900s, La Villita was almost a slum until 1939 when, under the leadership of Mayor Maury Maverick, the city began work on the San Antonio River Walk development. Fortunately, La Villita was restored building by building into a charming historic village that stands as a monument to San Antonio's rich past. This restored "La Villita" is dedicated to the preservation of early Texas and Spanish culture and the continuing education and promotion of arts and crafts. It is almost a replica of an Old Mexico cobblestone village. Some of these galleries and gift shops located in the restored historic buildings have been there for decades.

A walking tour of La Villita is the best way to explore the village, and it will take half a day. Art is definitely alive in La Villita. Galleries offer a variety of artwork, ranging from contemporary to southwest and Mexican folk art. One of the few remaining glass blowers in the country can be found in the village, and stained glass and jewelry artisans are available for custom work. You will find everything from hand-woven blankets and hand-thrown pottery to Bonsai trees and cowboy hats.

Of course, no visit to La Villita would be complete without seeing the beautiful Arneson River Theatre and the Little Church of La Villita.

Erected in 1939, the unique **Arneson River Theatre** is an outside stage on one side of the river, and grassy, stepped seating on the opposite side. During the summer, the Arneson takes on a Mexican flavor with entertainment almost every evening at Fiesta Noche Del Rio, Fiesta Flamenca and Fandango. Visitors are treated to bright, colorful costumes, flamenco guitars, Folklorico dance and Mariachis.

The **Little Church of La Villita**, with its Gothic revival architecture was built in 1879 and was acquired by the City of San Antonio in 1945. The lancet-shaped casement windows and hand-carved pegs were made by a Norwegian sailor. The small historic church is open daily, with church services twice a week, but is usually booked for weddings on Saturdays.

Market Square (The Mexican Market and El Mercado)

The romance and color of Old Mexico swirls through the streets of San Antonio's Market Square between West Commerce, Santa Rosa and Dolorosa. El Mercado offers exciting and festive shopping and dining in the city. Historic Market Square resembles an authentic Mexican market, complete with festive Tejano music and bright, bold treasures for the entire family. You can enjoy sizzling fajitas and homemade Mexican pastries in one of the famous Mexican Market patio restaurants, and browse the booths of El Mercado and the Farmers Market Plaza for great gifts and souvenirs.

Southtown

This lively, rather quirky section of downtown offers some of the city's best shopping, dining and excitement. It is a city revitalization project that includes the famous King William Historic District, the Blue Star Arts Complex and Lavaca, San Antonio's oldest existing neighborhood. The area lies just south of The Alamo, between Durango, South St. Mary's, South Presa, Flores and Probandt and is a unique mixture of historical houses, converted warehouses, art galleries, museums and restaurants. After a morning of shopping Southtown galleries and shops enjoy lunch at the adorable and funky Madhatters Tea House & Café or coffee at Casa Chiapas. Look into the San Antonio Conservation Society's walking tour for a great insight into this unique area, or take a Blue Trolley from downtown or the Riverwalk.

King William Historical District

Save time during your visit to discover San Antonio's most beautiful historic neighborhood—the King William Historical

District. Located just south of downtown on the east bank of the San Antonio River, the King William Historical District was established during the 1840s by a group of German immigrants and received the distinction, in 1967, of becoming Texas' first Historic Neighborhood District. The 25-square-block area was once farmland that belonged to the Mission San Antonio de Valero (The Alamo).

Mr. Ernst Altgelt, the first person to build a stately mansion on King William Street is credited with naming the street after King Wilhelm I of Prussia. Most of the homes were built in the Greek Revival, Victorian or Italianate styles, and even though most are privately owned, a few, like The Guenther House (1860) and the Edward Steves Homestead (1870) are open to the public for tours. From its early days when the area was settled until today the King William area has been noted as a very wealthy and distinguished neighborhood. The tree-lined streets, magnificent mansions and manicured gardens are unlike any in the entire city. Stop in at the office of the San Antonio Conservation Society, 107 King William St., for a self-guided walking tour guide booklet.

UPTOWN LOOP

Alamo Heights and **Terrell Hills** are actually cities within a city. Both have their own police departments and fire stations and children attend schools within the Alamo Heights School District. These neighborhoods make up the 78209 zip code, and the citizens have been dubbed "09'ers." These are cities rich in history and tradition, with thriving business districts, but they are some of the nicest business owners and residents you will meet in San Antonio. From ritzy and glitzy to cozy and quaint, you will love exploring the many boutiques, trendy shops and one-of-a-kind eateries that make up the "09" area of San Antonio. Inside this book you will read about the historic building that houses the antiques of Don Yarton, a collection of five wonderful stores called Rooms and Gardens, the upscale gift shop Hanley Wood, a lifesaving monogram gift shop called Memory Lane and so many other fine businesses.

This Uptown Broadway area includes many of San Antonio's top tourist attractions such as the San Antonio Zoo, the Japanese Tea Gardens, the Witte Museum, the McNay Art Institute, Brackenridge

26 A LADY'S DAY OUT IN SAN ANTONIO AND SURROUNDING AREAS – VOL. II

Park, the Botanical Gardens, and the unique Quarry Market and Golf Course. Shopping areas such as The Collection, The Carousel, the Sunset Ridge Shopping Center, and Broadway (the main street), are all located within the "Alamo Heights" community—a great place to visit and shop.

The **Monte Vista** National Historical District, just north of downtown includes impressive homes built in the Queen Anne, Georgian, Victorian or Moorish architecture from 1890-1930, and includes several bed and breakfasts and eclectic shops. The **Olmos Park** neighborhood dates back to 1920 when oilman and real estate tycoon H.C. Thorman bought the property from an Austrian count. It is just north of Hildebrand Avenue and east of San Pedro, and it, too, includes many wonderful places to shop and dine. From upscale linens and fine antiques to couture consignment and neighborhood soda fountains you can spend a day shopping this charming San Antonio community.

San Antonio Fairs Festivals & Fun

- For an up-to-date Calendar of Events, visit www.sanantoniocvb.com. Or, call the San Antonio Convention and Visitors Bureau at 210-207-6700 or 800-447-3372.

- Find complete Fiesta information at www.fiesta-sa.org or call 210-227-5191 or 877-723-4378.

- For more information on Southtown, contact the Southtown Mainstreet Alliance at 210-226-0888 or visit www.southtown.net.

- The King William Association can be contacted at www.kingwilliamassociation.org.

- Visit www.lavillita.com for additional information about La Villita Historic Arts Village.

Antiques & Interiors

Off My Rocker

The "thrill of the hunt" is partly what led Jo Lynn Swint to open Off My Rocker, 204 W. Olmos Dr. Starting with only a trailer full of antiques and collectibles in a co-op market booth, Jo Lynn accepted the challenge of opening her own shop. With courage and dedication, she has built her business into a very successful antique and consignment store in Olmos Park, adjoining Monte Vista, two of San Antonio's most charming neighborhoods. You will love browsing through this collection of amazing treasures. Off My Rocker is a mixture of delightful and unusual pieces of furniture, lighting, art, rugs and collectibles. New consignment items arrive daily. Jo Lynn is a savvy entrepreneur who has been featured in *San Antonio Woman* magazine. She is dedicated to giving you the best selection and the best service. "I have a sale every day," she says. "Come see for yourself!" Call 210-826-0250.

DON YARTON ANTIQUES

Opulent, stunning, dramatic. These are among the first words that come to mind the moment you enter Don Yarton Antiques & Accessories in San Antonio. Recently moved from his long time downtown location to 5424 Broadway, Don Yarton has found the perfect setting for his incredible fine antiques and furnishings. The site is a historic Mobil station at the corner of Broadway and Austin Hwy. that has become an Alamo Heights landmark. The iron "Pegasus" atop the building has a historic designation and belongs to the San Antonio Conservation Society. Through the years the building has housed many businesses, but for the first time seems to have found its perfect partner—a collection of magnificent 17th, 18th and 19th century antique treasures.

An 18th century day bed, canopied in Aubergine toile holds center stage in the main room (complete with a matching canopied doggie bed!). An entry table showcases a grouping of beautiful blue lamps—Persian, Imari and Chinese Mirror Blue; distinguished bronzes top marble columns; and massive armoires hold porcelains and candelabras. With these magnificent antique treasures Don has created a remarkable showroom filled with the elegance and grace of another time. He has covered the walls with exquisite 17th and 18th century French and Flemish tapestries and hung striking chandeliers throughout the rooms. In fact, many of the chandeliers are Don's own creation, some from parts of his own collection.

San Antonians have long associated the name Don Yarton with excellence. He has furnished beautiful homes from coast to coast, and his work has been featured in national magazines like *Veranda, Southern Living* and *Vogue.* For information call 210-821-5424 or visit www.donyarton.com.
(See related story page 9.)

Rooms and Gardens

Rooms filled with extraordinary treasures for the home and a tranquil garden filled with beautiful blooms, Rooms and Gardens, 5405 Broadway, is an elegant space occupied by five respected artists/owners with antiques and interiors that complement their different talents and styles.

Laurie Saunders, Ltd. is a sophisticated collection of fine antiques and interiors—a beautiful blend of old and new. Laurie likes the mix of Louis Philip chests, blue and white porcelains, Oriental accents, and African touches through rugs or pillows. She also carries Votivo and Sada France candles.

A Little Room – Owner Sherrie Sanderson's love for 17th, 18th and 19th century antiques and textiles influences her selection of beautiful European pieces such as Goblin wall tapestries and antique Turkish rugs. Especially remarkable are her lamps created from antique bases and shades in everything from Fortuny to French needlepoint.

Cartouche – Wende Quintanilla brings a rustic Spanish flair to the collection of rooms with antique and reproduction furniture, lamps and accessories. Unique items from Europe and Mexico like painted chests, candlesticks and Retablos (19th century devotional art).

Baker's is another "room" filled with furniture, pottery and accessories with a strong Brazilian influence. Sue Baker has a collection of remarkable pieces ranging from iron chandeliers to hand-painted furniture, as well as lots of oversized pieces for large rooms.

Architectural Elements – Walter Baker's space is painted a dark chocolate brown—perfect for his handsome framed artwork, horn mounts, overstuffed leather furniture and rare architectural elements that include mantles, consoles, and iron gates. Don't miss the great suede and leather gun cases and bird bags.

For additional information on all these great shops, call 210-829-5511.

Broadway & 9th Antiques

Locals will remember Broadway & 9th Antiques as the old Chrysler dealership, which was built in the 1930s. Today, it is one of San Antonio's most interesting and impressive places to shop for fabulous antiques and collectibles. Carmen Ingram fell in love with and purchased the building at 900 Broadway St., nine blocks north of The Alamo, in 1995. She and husband Bryant, along with daughter JoAnn Fox, began to renovate the historic space. JoAnn says, "My children were young, so I would bring them with me. For them it was 50,000 square feet of rollerblade heaven."

While Carmen and Bryant traveled throughout the world for antiques, JoAnn and her children scoured garage sales and estate sales for treasures. What makes the store such a success is that you will find a little of everything—old, new, rustic, garden, western, architectural and Shabby Chic. In fact, Broadway & 9th Antiques is such a treasure trove that it has drawn the attention of movie companies and marketing firms, which lease furnishings for movies and commercials. Interior Designers from across San Antonio, as well as the state have found Broadway & 9th Antiques to be the place to find that special piece.

The first floor is filled with wonderful items, including antiques, primitives, jewelry, vintage clothing, china and crystal and great artwork. Climb the ramp to the second floor and you'll find great bargains. Every time you visit, you'll find something new.

Carmen and JoAnn still work together in managing the store. Lovey and Richard have been a part of the team since the shop opened and recently, JoAnn's daughter Hillary has also joined the group. Their hard work, eye for detail and wonderful customer service has made Broadway & 9th a long-time favorite San Antonio locale where customers can find incredible bargains on quality antiques and collectibles. Call 210-223-2095.

As a child, Tonie Cortez loved collecting things. As an adult, she spent more than 30 years in corporate America. When the opportunity arose for her to combine her love of collecting with her business savvy, she jumped at it. As the owner of Alamo Antique Mall in San Antonio, she now has one of the largest "collections" in Texas. Just two blocks from its famous namesake—The Alamo—Alamo Antique Mall, 125 Broadway St., is the city's largest antique mall. Built in 1866, the historic three-story building once housed several businesses. It's now the absolute perfect home for this huge collection of antiques and collectibles. Showcasing collections from 75 merchants, you will be delighted with the plethora of art, glass, estate jewelry, vintage clothing, rare coins, war memorabilia, records and silver. Plan to spend lots of time in this antique paradise. There are so many rooms to explore, and so many treasures to discover. Whether you are looking for a particular piece of crystal, a vintage handbag, a 1950s lunch box or even a framed original poster of Paul McCartney (yes, I found it and bought it), you will love poking through all three floors. Call 210-224-4354.

THE COTTAGE ANTIQUES

From the welcoming red sign to the enticing treasures found within and the warm customer service, you're sure to fall in love with The Cottage Antiques. One of San Antonio's premier antique shops is located at 239 W. Sunset Rd. in a quaint Alamo Heights' bungalow filled with upscale antique furniture and accessories. Owner Cheryl Jelinski and her daughter Jennifer work closely with their dealers to provide a large selection of fine antiques for their customers. They carry 18th-20th century American and European antiques—everything from primitive to formal. New merchandise arrives daily, so visit often to see the constantly changing displays throughout the shop. There is also a large selection of fine antique paintings that will provide the perfect accent to any home. Call 210-930-2811.

LASTING IMPRESSIONS ANTIQUES

Near the historic neighborhood of Olmos Park, you will find a wonderful antique store that will definitely make a "Lasting Impression!" Owner Carmen Morin started her antique business in 1982 in a small space—her garage—but Lasting Impressions Antiques, 600 W. Hildebrand, has since grown into one of San Antonio's most respected antique stores. Antiques and collectibles range from very affordable to high end, in styles like Shabby Chic, refined European and more. Multiple rooms hold beautiful furniture pieces, stunning light fixtures and magnificent artwork. Carmen also offers in-home consultations and restoration and refinishing services. Carmen and her staff love the business, know their customers and aim to please. Call 210-737-9130 for more information.

Artists & Art Galleries

The Village Gallery

Professional potters Walt and Cynthia Glass have been creating beautiful, vibrant ceramic pottery since the opening of their gallery in 1972. The Village Gallery is one of the many wonderful shops in La Villita, San Antonio's first neighborhood. In fact, from 1898-1917 this shop housed St. Phillips College. Walt and Cynthia are both generational Texans whose ancestors fought at the Alamo for Texas' independence. They graduated from the University of the Incarnate Word in San Antonio with degrees in art. Walt and Cynthia are passionate about their work and are nationally and internationally known for their colorful stoneware and porcelain pottery. They typically use materials from local sources to mix their own clay and glaze and often are found visiting with customers in the Gallery. While Walt and Cynthia's main studio is in McQueeney, Texas, The Village Gallery, 502 Villita St. is where they showcase their work along with that of other artists. Call 210-226-0404 or visit www.mcqueeneypottery.com.

If you are not already familiar with Donna Dobberfuhl, you will be in the very near future. A professional studio sculptor since 1973, Donna is best known in San Antonio for her 35-foot-tall, 50-foot-wide sculpture called "Christ Ascending and Welcoming All" in St. Mark the Evangelist Catholic Church. She is also nationally recognized for her design and placement of sculptures throughout the United States in botanical gardens, government agencies, museums, civic and education facilities and churches. This includes a 98-foot-long brick rendition of the 14 Stations of the Cross for St. Thomas the Apostle Church in Staten Island, N.Y. But, locals will soon recognize her name as the author of a proposal to create a panoramic, three-dimensional parade of animals along both sides of U.S. 281 near the San Antonio Zoo. Donna's plans include a representation of cultures from prehistoric times to the present with her "river" of animals and symbols. You can view the plans for this exciting project in her local studio and gallery.

Donna Dobberfuhl's studio, "Sculptural Designs Atelier," is located at 1514 Broadway St., and is a must visit for both San Antonio locals and visitors. This sculptor graduated cum laude with an MFA degree from The New York Academy of Art Graduate School of Figurative Art. She has studied the masters in Europe, and is a professional member of the National Sculpture Society. She specializes in the sculpture of architectural brick, fine art bronze, fabricated metal and custom tile making her one of the most sought after and notable sculptors of our time. Donna's works have been featured on CBS's Sunday Morning, CNN, Fox News, The Discovery Channel and Texas Country Reporter. Please visit www.sculpturaldesigns.com or call 210-224-0220 for your masterpiece.

VILLITA STAINED GLASS
Stained Glass • Gift Shop

Watching light delicately stream through an exquisite piece of stained glass captivates the imagination. In fact, that beauty has held Roy and Gerry Ledenham's attention for more than 40 years. In 1982, these talented artisans opened Villita Stained Glass in the charming collection of shops known as La Villita. The building that houses their shop is actually one of the oldest buildings in La Villita, built in 1873. Villita Stained Glass, at 418 Villita, offers incredible kaleidoscopes, sun-catchers, sculptures, prisms, treasure boxes and candleholders. Today, Roy and Gerry's daughter, Melvillyn Adame, carries on the family tradition, managing this brilliant shop. Visitors can even watch Melvillyn craft beautiful glass beads for jewelry in the studio a couple of days a week. For more information about Villita Stained Glass, call 210-223-4480 or visit www.lavillita.com.

Attractions & Entertainment

SAS Shoemakers Village is home to one of the few remaining shoe manufacturers in the United States. SAS was founded in 1976 by two shoemakers from Maine who, on a shoestring budget, fulfilled their dream of creating fine shoes in America. Today, after more than three decades of quality craftsmanship and unsurpassed customer service, SAS is known for producing a wide selection of handcrafted leather shoes for men, women and toddlers, as well as an array of stylish handbags.

At the heart of Shoemaker's Village is a General Store where the smell of hot, buttery popcorn mixed with the aroma of freshly brewed coffee and warm cookies, extends a warm welcome. Adjoining the General Store is a wonderful old barn with a 30-foot ceiling. Barn cats and roosters peer down from the loft at the wonderful assortment of fun. There are vintage cars, shelves filled with antiques, an Ice Cream Parlor with authentic swivel stools from Woolworth's five-and-dime and a Candy Store with dozens of old-time sweets.

The unique blend of a friendly atmosphere and quality footwear wins the hearts and "soles" of SAS visitors. For more information or to schedule a tour of the SAS Factory in San Antonio at 101 New Laredo Hwy., call 210-924-6507 or visit www.sasshoes.com. *(Color photo featured in front section of book.)*

Bakeries

THE ULTIMATE CHEESECAKE BAKERY

When Mary Jane Ontiveroz's parents gave her a beginning cake decorating kit over 30 years ago, he had no idea that such a simple gift would become a lifelong pursuit. But indeed it has! And, San Antonio is all the better for it. Mary Jane's artistry has captured national attention on CNN and in two national magazines. She and her husband Thomas, a private chef in his spare time, own The Ultimate Cheesecake Bakery. This wonderful bakery tempts the tummy with its wide assortment of freshly baked cookies, luscious pies and more than 35 mouth-watering flavors of cheesecakes. So good—it was even voted San Antonio's best dessert and bakery by AolCityGuide.com in 2007. Mary Jane and Thomas offer many samples right in the store. For the "Ultimate Cheesecake" experience, contact either of the two locations; in Alamo Heights, call 210-826-1505; or in North San Antonio, call 210-494-5496, or stop by 17700 US Hwy. 281 N. Visit www.ultimateweddingcake.com.

Bed & Breakfasts

Alamo City's Little Flower Inn

Just two blocks from San Antonio's Pasaeo del Rio, a short walk to the Alamo, and right in the middle of San Antonio's elegant King William Historic District, you'll find the perfect bed and breakfast getaway! Alamo City's Little Flower Inn, 225 Madison St., blooms with great style and charm, a big front porch and a second floor balcony. The Innkeepers' first priority is for each guest to feel pampered and comfortable. With full run of the entire house expect a true one-of-a-kind experience. All rooms have access to a screened-in porch, cabana or balcony, and each is decorated with beautiful antiques. A breakfast basket filled with delicious treats is delivered to your room each morning, and you just may want to enjoy it in the beautiful flowering garden or the pool area. The garden is also a perfect setting for intimate weddings or parties. Escape to the "elegant side of San Antonio" at Alamo City's Little Flower Inn. For more information, call 210-354-3116 or visit www.littleflowerinn.com. *(Color photo featured in front section of book.)*

ARBOR HOUSE SUITES

Clustered around exquisite gardens just blocks from the famous River Walk and La Villita Historic Arts Village, the great heritage of old San Antonio can be found at Arbor House Suites. Owner Ron Stinson opened the Arbor House Suites in 2002, but the history of the four building complex dates back to the turn-of-the-20th-century when a Swiss cabinetmaker built the cottage homes for his family. Ron was attending church nearby when his daughter saw that one of the buildings was for sale. When he inquired about the sale, he found that all four buildings were to be auctioned. He bought the entire complex and began renovations that have earned a San Antonio Conservation Society plaque for excellence in historic renovations.

Each house is named for a Texas river that had significance in the independence of Texas, and each suite bears the name of an Alamo hero. Ron himself is a fifth generation Texan, and a member of the Sons of the Republic of Texas. His passion and knowledge of Texas history is apparent in the Arbor House Suites. This warm, rich bed and breakfast, which was featured in Southern Living magazine, has been decorated with beautiful art and furniture. Each house has three suites featuring high ceilings, pine wood floors, private baths and home amenities, including a refrigerator, a microwave, and a coffee pot. There are also TVs, phones with voicemail and free Wi-Fi. A continental breakfast is delivered to your suite each morning in a delightful picnic basket, and you can enjoy it in the wonderful "secret garden" atmosphere of the courtyard. For information or reservations, call 210 472 2005, 888-272-6700 or visit www.arborhouse.com. This Bed and Breakfast garden oasis, 109 Arciniega St., is "Texas at Its Finest!"

Don and Liesl Noble love San Antonio... and they should! Their families have been an integral part of this community for more than 100 years. In fact, Don's great-great-great grandparents, Samuel and Mary Maverick, were the first American couple to settle in the city. Samuel was even sent to sign the Texas Declaration of Independence for the Alamo's defenders!

So it's no surprise that this couple has worked to preserve a bit of the history that makes this city great. In 1991, Don converted his family's carriage house into a three-room bed & breakfast. The home, the **Aaron Pancoast Carriage House**, at 202 Washington St., was originally built in 1896 for Don's great-grandfather. It offers wonderful privacy, a full-size swimming pool and heated spa. Then in 1995, Don and Liesl purchased **The Jackson House**, at 107 Madison St., a charming Victorian home from 1894 that has lovely gardens and a heated swim-spa. And finally, in 2004, they purchased **The Ogé House**, a rare, ante-bellum Greek Revival mansion that was originally built in 1857. The Ogé House, at 209 Washington St., sits on San Antonio's famed Riverwalk and has 10 rooms. These three lovely, historic homes make up Noble Inns. They are situated within a block of each other in San Antonio's downtown King William Historic District.

Each house has been lovingly restored to its original, distinct glory. Beautiful European antiques take you back in time, and modern amenities like high-speed Internet, flexible breakfast options and business services make your stay even more enjoyable. And for an extra special treat, consider reserving a ride in the Nobles' 1960 Rolls Royce Silver Cloud II. It's just another example of the first-class service that waits for you at Noble Inns. For more information, call 210-223-2353, 800-221-4045 or visit www.nobleinns.com. *(Featured on front cover and in color section of the book.)*

Fashion & Accessories

Friends Kathy Hoermann (well known in San Antonio for her Painted Pony clothing line and store) and Alexa Thornton (owner of a Curves exercise facility and a former fashion illustrator) have joined talents in creating San Antonio's very unique consignment boutique—Otra Vez Couture Consignment. Located at 145 W. Olmos Dr. in the charming Olmos Park neighborhood, Otra Vez ("Once Again") is gaining respect for its fabulous designer clothing at incredibly low prices. Discover high-end clothing, accessories and jewelry by top designers such as Chanel, Escada, Louis Vuitton, Valentino, Armani, Dior, Ralph Lauren, Ferragamo, Burberry, DKNY, Louis Féraud and many more. Their goal as a "green store" is to provide an exciting place to shop for outstanding merchandise, and to help clients get a return on their investment. Visit www.otravezconsignment.com or call 210-826-0606 for information. Remarkable prices for designer fashion clothing—Otra Vez!

Florists

Alamo Plants and Petals

With its irresistible tablescapes, intoxicating blooms and unique silk flower creations, Alamo Plants and Petals, 119 W. Sunset Rd., has been recognized as a premier San Antonio florist since opening its doors in 1979. Having been featured in various publications like *San Antonio Weddings*, *The Knot* and *San Antonio Woman*, the store offers an array of exquisite flowers from around the world and event planning services for parties and weddings. Customers know they can trust the award-winning design staff with their most important celebrations. And while the store is always stunning, you'll definitely want to drop by during the holidays when it's especially breathtaking. For more information, visit www.alamoplantsandpetals.com or call 210-828-2628, 800-776-9821.

Gifts & Home Décor

Whether you need a centerpiece for your table, a seasonal wreath for your front door or floral arrangements for a special event, the talented floral designers at Saturday Market can fill the order. Located at 4704 Broadway in Alamo Heights, Saturday Market is San Antonio's source for custom silk floral arrangements. Eric Mitchell and Felix Morales will work with your specifications to create the perfect floral arrangements for your special needs. If you need a little help with seasonal decorations for your office or themed décor for that special event, Saturday Market will create a wonderful design. The shop has also become a favorite place to shop for home décor, accessories, candles, holiday decorations and gifts. And, you'll love meeting the two resident canine greeters and assistants! For more information, call 210-731-9525.

HANLEY·WOOD
Fine Giftware & Bridal Registry

Thirty-five years ago Annabell Ames went against the wishes and warnings of everyone in her family to take a very small inheritance and open her first retail store. Hanley Wood, 5611 Broadway St., has evolved into one of San Antonio's premier gift and home boutiques. The building itself is charming, with interesting architecture and great lighting. Incredible displays throughout the store include exquisite crystal, china, silver and decorative tabletop pieces.

Many San Antonio brides consider Hanely Wood their main or only wedding registry. The friendly and knowledgeable staff not only walks them through the process of wedding selection and registry, but offers valuable design and entertaining advice as well.

For the table, you'll find beautiful selections of china, crystal and flatware. Hanley Wood carries lovely lines of china including Versace and Meissen. Its crystal line sparkles with names like Simon Pearce and Nambé, and its sterling flatware like Buccellati, will make your table even more elegant. Entertaining with pieces by Annie Modica, Arthur Court and Wilson Armetale will make every event special.

The entire store is a stunning collection of fine and beautiful items for the table and bar, but you will also find wonderful gifts for babies such as silver porringers, picture frames and rattles. And of course, Hanley Wood is the perfect place to shop for unique gifts for special people. There is a wonderful line of items made just for Texans who know how to entertain with "style!"

Shop online at www.hanleywoodtexas.com or call 210-822-3311. There is also a second Hanley Wood store in Corpus Christi.

Robin Sherrington had more than 28 years in retail experience with Marshall Field's, Bering's and Neiman-Marcus—so she was a natural when it came to owning her own gift and decorative accessory store. Robin's Nest is a beautiful store in the heart of Olmos Park at 4216 McCullough Ave. in San Antonio, filled with remarkable home décor, quality furniture and unique gifts. Everything is artfully displayed and is a delight in which to browse. Robin carries John Richards furniture, and has a large selection of beautiful Talavera pottery. You'll find handsome pewter serving pieces, stunning tabletop decorations and much more. The staff is extremely friendly and eager to help "feather your nest" with the perfect decorative piece. Call 210-930-6378 or visit www.shoprobinsnest.com.

Pampered Pets

The minute you walk through the door of this wonderful pet store you will be greeted by the sweet sounds of chirping birds, a friendly smile and maybe even the resident "store kitty." Pet Works, 6446 N. New Braunfels Ave., is located in San Antonio's historic Sunset Ridge Shopping Center in Alamo Heights, where it has been a local favorite for many years. Owner and pet lover Sheila Crane has been in the pet business since 1989, and is dedicated to providing the very best pets, products and service to her customers. As a Certified Avian Specialist, Sheila offers many varieties of locally bred, hand-raised baby birds, and behavior consultations for parrots. You'll find birdcages to suit every budget and style, as well as pet products for every animal type. From aquariums, collars, and bedding, to premium dog and cat foods and even decorative cookie treats, this fun store definitely has "the works!" For more information, call 210-824-6634.

Photography

Photographers
FINE PORTRAITURE

When Dorothy Langmore first opened her photography studio in 1984, she was a newly single mother of three just trying to make ends meet. Little did she know that her impressionistic-style photos would become so well respected in the industry or that she would one day take pictures of Hollywood legends like Eva Gabor, Farrah Fawcett and Ellyn Burstyn. She had even less of an idea that she and her former husband, also an avid photographer, would inspire their children to follow in their footsteps. But that is exactly what happened.

Langmore is best known for its soft ethereal-style and timeless black and white portraits. Today, a second generation of Langmores has continued the tradition of capturing the essence of life in pictures. After years of hearing photography discussed at the dinner table, the Langmore children couldn't help but be bitten by the photography bug. Will and Marie now manage the studio, and have brought their own signature styles to the family business. Will is especially talented at capturing candid, interpersonal interaction shots with children. Marie is best known for her maternally-instinctive mother-daughter portraits and images of pregnant women. John, an attorney by trade, even shoots photography in his spare time. With so much talent and such varying styles, it's no surprise that Langmore has become a mainstay for many Texas families, immortalizing those precious family moments that everyone wants to remember.

Langmore Photography is located at 5800 Broadway St. in the Alamo Heights area of San Antonio. Call 210-826-6300 or visit www.langmore.com.

Restaurants, Tea Houses & Coffee Houses

Located in the heart of Southtown and the King William District, Casa Chiapas, 926 S. Alamo St., is one of the most interesting and unique restaurants and coffee houses. (In fact, it has been featured as the backdrop for several films currently in production.) Mother and son owners Mary and Eddie, Jr. Martinez serve coffee made from organically grown beans imported from Chiapas, Mexico, to help support the people from that region. Mary and Eddie have such sweet spirits it's always a delight to be greeted by one or both. Husband, father and partner, Eddie, Sr., also joins the gang to make it a true family affair. Breakfasts include delicious omelets, pancakes and, of course, huevos rancheros and chilaquiles. For lunch or dinner try a great salad, sandwich wrap or warm Panini. Throughout the house, you'll find jewelry, purses, shirts and table runners—all handmade, and a selection of original artwork by up and coming artists. Guests are entertained by local musicians, including Eddie, Jr. himself, who is quite an accomplished guitarist. Coffee, tea, breakfast, lunch, dessert, music, art, jewelry, new friends—what a great place to visit on your Lady's Day Out! Call 210-224-2606 or visit www.casachiapassa.net.

You will be "mad as a March Hare" for the absolutely wonderful, Madhatters Tea House & Café. This is not the typical teahouse. It is a bright, fun and magical place where you almost expect to see Alice herself sipping tea with a dormouse! Owner/Chef Rene Guerrero opened the Tea House in 1995 in San Antonio, and then moved to the heart of the King William Historic District, 320 Beauregard, in 2001. Madhatters Tea House & Café is open seven days a week serving an eclectic breakfast, lunch and dinner.

Select your own teacup and choose from more than 50 varieties of handpicked loose teas, or sip on one of seven different organic and fair-trade iced teas each day. Breakfast, lunch and dinner are served daily, or you may bring in the little ones for a delightful Kids Tea. Afternoon Tea and High Teas are available anytime of day, with a variety of delicious tea sandwiches, fresh-baked scones and petits fours.

Tea is also used in many of Rene's original recipes. The house dressing is blackberry tea vinaigrette, the chicken breast is smoked with Lapsang Souchong Tea, and the Mushroom Ravioli is served with a tea-smoked garlic broth at dinnertime. Everything is delicious! Madhatters also features an eclectic wine and beer list, and they even have a small wine shop and gift store.

Don't miss an experience in one of San Antonio's most beloved Tea Houses. It is the perfect place for a ladies day out, a business lunch, or a bridal or baby shower. "We are proud that Madhatters Tea House & Café has been featured in *National Geographic*, *Traveler*, *The New York Times*, *City Search*, *San Antonio Magazine* and *Texas Monthly*," says Rene. For more information, call 210-212-4832 or visit www.madhatterstea.com

Specialty Shops

Memory Lane
Monograms & Gifts

We love absolutely everything about this charming store—from the clever name and unusual gift items to the welcoming smiles from the owner and her sweet family! Lane Hooton left the accounting world (after much prayer) to open Memory Lane, and the store has fast become a local favorite in the Alamo Heights area of San Antonio. It is a bright and colorful space, filled with wonderful items that are perfect for any occasion. Personalization is what truly makes this store unique. Lane can monogram, etch or engrave almost everything she sells—from garment bags to cocktail napkins, sterling silver to glassware, baby blankets to toys. Memory Lane is a delightful place to shop for the perfect personalized gift and even meet new friends. Be sure to say hello to Lane, her mother, cousin and dear friend. Even Lane's dad joins in the fun. "It is definitely a family affair," Lane admits. "We have so much fun playing and meeting new people." Just one stop to 5800 Broadway St., and we're sure you'll be hooked too! For more information, call 210-828-4800.

Discover
North Central
San Antonio /
Bulverde / Bracken

North of 410, including Loop 1604, between IH-10 and IH-35, is another unique section of San Antonio, where wonderful treasures await your discovery.

The far north central area of San Antonio is growing at a fast pace, and includes several more upscale neighborhoods such as The Dominion, Sonterra, Thousand Oaks and Stone Oak. Many of San Antonio's rich and famous call these areas home, including America's favorite country crooner, George Strait, and many of the San Antonio Spurs including David Robinson, Tony Parker, Manu Ginobili, Tim Duncan, Bruce Bowen and Coach Gregg Popovich.

Chic, fashionable and trendy describe these north central San Antonio neighborhoods and its shopping opportunities. From Castle Hills' shops on the west border to Stone Oak boutiques to the east, you'll need a few days to see it all. Be sure to save time to shop the beautiful new La Cantera shopping center, a collection of high-end stores and restaurants off IH-10 near Fiesta Texas. Here is where you will find big name stores like Nordstrom and Neiman Marcus.

For all-in-the-family entertainment, San Antonio's two famous theme parks, SeaWorld and Fiesta Texas are located in this north central area and draw visitors from around the world. A visit to each of these attractions will take an entire day, but will be well worth the time. From Shamu and water rides to scary roller coasters and theme musicals, both parks are filled with entertainment for all ages.

Bulverde, a small rural community bordered on the south by San Antonio, Boerne on the west, and New Braunfels on the east, is becoming more and more a "great escape" for the city folks who are looking for peace and quiet, and relaxation. Locals really hope they can keep Bulverde a secret a little longer, but that will be difficult because it is such a charming town.

Its history is connected to the early days of Fredericksburg, when in 1836 a road was built to connect it to New Braunfels. This road went through what is now downtown Bulverde, which was once called "The Village." The actual settlement of Bulverde was founded in 1850 as a stopping point for travelers, and named for one of the early landowners, Luciano Bulverdo. The rugged Hill Country land was once home to many American Indian tribes including Tonkawa, Karankawa, and Lipan. Arrowheads can still be found today at one location called Bulverde Point.

Visitors to Bulverde love the slow, gentle pace of the town, the warm hospitality of the business owners and, of course, the wonderful treasures they discover. In fact, Bulverde is becoming known as "wrought iron alley." Stop along Highway 281 North and find acres of unique iron pieces and beautiful pottery for the home and garden, all at great bargains. (You can't miss them!)

Outdoor enthusiasts will appreciate great opportunities for fun along the Guadalupe River and the hilly terrain. The Upper Guadalupe River is a favorite place for tubing, canoeing and fishing, and Guadalupe State Park is one of the state's most beautiful state parks. It has four miles of river frontage, and is a temporary home-away-from-home for many RV travelers.

If you visit during the spring or fall you might be lucky enough to be part of the festival held the third Sunday in May and the third Sunday in October. This community celebration is held in the historic Anhalt Building, which was built in 1875 to house the German farm club called "Die Germaina Farmer Verein." It is family-style food, music, dancing and a great time for all.

Just north of Loop 1604 out Nacogdoches Road you'll find the adorable shopping enclave called "**Bracken Village.**" It is a beautiful 10-acre collection of masterfully restored homes that house intriguing gift shops and businesses. Bracken Village got its start during the 1980s when an artist/antique collector and historical preservationist purchased the land and began to refurbish the original three homes on the property. Artisans and business owners began to find the charming Bracken Village and today there are more than 15 different shops and boutiques located under the majestic oaks.

Park your car and walk through the charming country cottages that house garden and jewelry shops and collections of antiques and fine gifts. Take your time to enjoy this unique group of fine shops, and then ask for directions to the almost famous Bracken Store Café. (It is rumored that a famous San Antonio movie star likes the hamburgers here!)

Bracken Village is a shopping treat any time of year, but during December Bracken Village becomes a "Dickens Village," complete with strolling musicians in period costumes, horse drawn carriages and carolers. You can step back in time and enjoy shopping and dining circa 1900!

The Bulverde/Spring Branch area Chamber of Commerce can be reached at 830-438-4285 or 866-BULVERDE (866-285-8373) or visit www.bulverdechamber.com.

Antiques & Interiors

Old Downtown Bulverde Emporium

Originally built as a bowling alley in the early 1920s, this building has also served as a feed store, a party room and a church youth center. Since 1984, however, Old Downtown Bulverde Emporium, has found its home here at 2355 Bulverde Rd. Filled top to bottom with incredible antiques, furniture, collectibles, art and gifts. You will find a lovely collection of original watercolors by Texas artists, linens, glassware, china, quilts, books and so much more. Located just one mile west of Hwy. 281 on Hwy. 1863. Call Nancy Benedetti at 830-438-2914.

Sweet Pea Cottage

Shabby Chic treasures, wonderful antiques, one-of-a-kind collectibles and fabulous gifts! You will find these and more at the adorable Sweet Pea Cottage. These lovely antique booths, located in Homestead Handcrafts at 4536 Thousand Oaks Dr. and 21518 Blanco Rd. in San Antonio are brimming with unique and fun gift items. Owner JaNell Hester displays cottage charm and chic style where you can find antique treasures, gifts, and other whimsical delights.

These booths are fun and enchanting with everything from Antiques and vintage finds to gifts for you and your pet. For more information, call 210-637-1842 or 210-402-1221. JaNell's signature style is one-of-a-kind. Great store, charming owner and fabulous finds! *(See related story on page 74.)*

Artists & Art

The Painted Plate

Ideal for celebrating a baby or bridal shower, birthday party, or just to satisfy the budding artist within, The Painted Plate is a great outlet for any level of artistic ability. This paint-it-yourself-pottery-shop, at 19141 Stone Oak Pkwy., in the Stone Oak area of San Antonio, is "where everyone is an artist." Owners Jane O'Neill and daughter Kelley Austin will help you choose from an assortment of items to paint. For more information, call 210-545-6886 or visit www.paintedplatestudio.com.

Children's

"Early beginnings make a world of difference." This is the motto and impetus behind the Aragon Spanish Academy, a Christian-based Spanish immersion preschool and after-school program, located at 18952 Redland Rd. in San Antonio. Husband and wife owners Rick and Rosa Linda Gonzales have developed a curriculum that introduces young children to the Spanish language in a caring and fun environment through song, play and art. For more information, visit www.aragonacademy.com or call 210-496-0990.

Fashion & Accessories

23 SKADOO

After selling her beautiful fashion and decorative items in craft shows and at Market Days for many years, Susan Moore happened upon the charming Bracken Village, just northeast of San Antonio, and knew it would be the perfect location for a store. Her festive shop, 23 Skadoo, is located at 18771 FM 2252, in a historic house that was moved from downtown to the Village. It is a perfect backdrop for her unique, art-inspired items, such as Laurel Burch purses and La tee Da effusion lamps and fragrance fuel. Susan features many of her own handmade items in the store, as well as others from regional artists. She has fabulous things for everyone from young teens to Red Hat Ladies—bags and totes, fun accessories and "wearable art." During the holidays Bracken Village is transformed into a Dickens Christmas, and Susan joins the other shop owners in period costume to greet her guests. Call 210-651-6512.

From the beautiful displays of quality women's clothing to the change jingling in your pocket when you leave, you will love everything about this premier resale boutique. Encore, 1931 NW Military Hwy. has been a number one choice for sophisticated San Antonio women since 1985. Owner Barbara Allison has an innate sense of style and infectious love of people that has enabled her business to stay current and successful through the years. Women love shopping at Encore because they know they will always find the latest trends and fashions, but at a fraction of the cost. Barbara consigns clothing from people across the country, so her inventory is very diverse and exciting. You will find traditional business attire, upscale formal wear and fun, festive ensembles, as well as designer purses, stunning jewelry and unique accessories. Ask any customer why they love shopping at Encore and they will tell you that in addition to the wonderful clothes at great prices, they love being treated like a close friend by the entire staff! For more information, call 210-341-0939.

Charmed by Gucci, Prada, Armani and other designer labels, yet intrigued by sophisticated savings? Then you'll love Baubles & Beads, 2267 NW Military Hwy. in San Antonio's Castle Hills area, where upscale resale is always in style. Owner Yana Kaplan, who emigrated from Russia when she was eight years old, carefully selects the finest seasonable, clean consignments. You will also find a great selection of purses, belts and jewelry to accessorize any ensemble, making this unique boutique a fashion gem. For more information, call 210-341-8491.

Furniture, Gifts & Home Décor

GARDEN FANTASY

This cozy, 19th century Bracken Village cottage is filled with wonderful treasures that will make any garden a beautiful fantasy retreat. Owner Kay Thomason and her husband, a Master Gardener, opened Garden Fantasy, 18771 FM 2252, in 2004. After years of traveling and working in health care (her) and general contracting (him), they decided to settle down. When Kay suddenly lost her husband, she decided to keep the shop as a testament to their love and dreams. It is the perfect place to find everything from unique magnetic mailbox covers and concrete turtles to vibrant Bougainvillea, Coleus and Gardenias. You will find a kaleidoscope of brilliant blooms and gifts for the house and garden. Kay carries metal stars in all sizes and colors, Woodstock precision-tuned wind chimes, Joan Baker stained glass, and a large selection of angels and crosses. Make your "Garden Fantasy" come true in this charming store. Call 210-651-4683.

Collector's Gallery
San Antonio's Largest and Finest Gift Shop
Since 1978

This amazing and beautiful gift gallery has held the honor of being San Antonio's largest gift shop since 1978. Collector's Gallery, located at 13500 West Ave. near W. Bitters Rd., is an elegant and sophisticated place filled with collectibles and treasures for every season. In fact, every day is Christmas at the Gallery with a spectacular collection of lines like Christopher Radko, Dept. 56, Mark Roberts Fairies, Byers Choice and Fontanini. You'll find everything you can possibly imagine to make your holidays happy and beautiful.

Collector's Gallery is family-owned-and-operated, and owner Jo Lynn Powell is as elegant and beautiful as her store. Her keen eye for detail and quality has allowed her to stay in touch with the latest, most popular lines in giftware. "We are different because we carry a large selection of all the lines we display," Jo Lynn says. You'll find beautiful collectible pieces by Lladro, MI Hummel, Jim Shore's Heartwood Creek, Willow Tree, Swarovski, Wee Forest Folk, Boyds Bears and Precious Moments. There is also a gift registry to make gift giving easy.

Beautiful displays of collectibles and gifts for every age fill the bright, spacious rooms. Fun lines include Webkinz, Jibbitz and Tea Posey. The Gallery is also the largest dealer for the very popular Crocs in every color for adults and children. You will also find a large selection of Lampe Berger, and fragrances that will fill your home with delicious scents. If Waterford is your passion, you'll find beautifully cut frames, perfume bottles, decanters and Christmas ornaments. And, the Vera Bradley selection is enormous! With more than 15,000 square feet, Jo Lynn has seen to it that her customers are in for an experience.

The friendly and knowledgeable staff is always available to assist you in finding the perfect gift for all the special people in your life. For more information, call 210-497-2525, 877-857-2356 or visit www.colgal.com. *(Color photo featured in front section of book.)*

Leslie & Co.
specializing in home accessories and gifts

Leslie & Co. is a breathtaking store with a unique array of home accessories, floral creations, linens, gifts and so much more. The previous owner, Leslie Hunt, opened the shop in 1992. Alyssa Myers, the store's new owner, is dedicated to offering the same timeless items and exceptional personal service that have been successful for the past 15 years. Along with the new ownership, fresh, new ideas and styles with a classic, modern flare abound.

Alyssa is committed to continuing the shop's high standard of excellence in both customer satisfaction and innovative merchandise. She is proud to say that Leslie & Co. will continue to be a "homegrown" company, locally owned, and reflecting the exquisite look and culture of San Antonio. Visit Leslie & Co. at 2165 NW Military Hwy., and let the "Leslie Girls" help you mix your special family treasures with new additions. For more information, call 210-349-1209.

Thank goodness humble beginnings don't have to stay humble. Hill Country Rustics first began selling rustic furniture on weekends in a small storefront, but when owner James Young purchased the small furniture store in 2004, he knew it had big potential. By July 2005 he and his team had found just the place, at 33000 Hwy. 281 N in Bulverde, to offer clients a great selection of quality furnishings at affordable prices. Specializing in home and office furniture and accessories, Hill Country Rustics offers furniture styles like Western Ranch, Country Elegant and Texas Tuscan. The store is decorated in stylish, designer-inspired vignettes so you can envision how the pieces could look in your home. Hill Country Rustics serves customers in San Antonio, Texas and throughout the entire United States. You'll especially love the luxurious leather furniture, fabulous artwork and outstanding service. Call 830-980-8998 or visit www.hillcountryrustic.com.

Bless Your Heart
Gift Shop and Boutique

This charming store is the result of a lifelong dream come true for sisters Katy Brockman and Rachel Dranselka. Located in an early 1900s house at 18771 FM 2252 in Bracken Village of San Antonio, this "girly girl paradise" has a lovely wrap-around front porch that is as welcoming as its owners. Stocked full of treasures—new and old—for you, your home and your garden, you're sure to find something you just must have. The sisters combined two stores into one, making Bless Your Heart Gift Shop & Boutique bigger, better and even more fabulous!

Born and raised in San Antonio, this dynamic duo (with much help from Mom and Dad) opened this trendy, fun shop for the young and young-at-heart. Katy and Rachel offer the very latest fashions in shoes, like Reef and Yellow Box; the hippest clothes, like Miss Me Jeans with plenty of sparkle; and unique t-shirts that you won't find anywhere else. The sisters also have a huge assortment of fun, fashion jewelry that can highlight any ensemble and any pocketbook.

If you're looking for a gift or something for your home, the girls at Bless Your Heart have you covered there, too! From Vera Bradley to Mary Engelbreit and seasonal décor, they have filled their store with treasures for every age. They always scour markets for unusual items. Their father has even restored some of the furniture—even though it usually required pink paint.

Katy and Rachel offer all of this (and more!) at prices that won't break the bank. New items arrive weekly, so the store is always changing. They also plan lots of "ladies' nights out" during the year, so grab a couple of girlfriends and treat yourself to a fun evening. You will love shopping here and meeting the sisters and their family. They will truly "Bless Your Heart!" Visit online www.shoppingismycardio.com or call 210-651-1000.

Bulverde Trading Post

It's a taste of the Hill Country with a wild Texas twist, and one of Bulverde's true local treasures. Bulverde Trading Post, 28890 Hwy. 281 N., is a must visit for unique gift items and home décor, but it's also a great place to soak up the down-home country atmosphere of this small Texas town. Owners Ronnie and Melissa Rogers were born and raised on South Texas ranches before moving to Bulverde, and they've filled the store with fabulous cowhides, deer horn lamps, wagons, wagon wheels, pottery and, of course, lots of Texas stars. They have created what they call a "down-home, countrified, get together, tell your big tales" type of atmosphere. Inventory changes all the time, so you'll find something new and unusual each time you visit. Call 830-438-7977, or just stop by with your own "tall tales!"

Jewelry & Beads

Get ready San Antonio! Get ready world! The young, energetic and incredibly talented Jenny Forks is setting the jewelry world on fire. She has developed quite a following of devoted customers and clients who absolutely love her artistic flair for handcrafted jewelry. What began as a small bead shop in Boerne in 2003 is now a successful store in San Antonio. Bitter Creek Designs, 17711 W. IH 10, is experiencing unprecedented recognition and growth. Jenny creates one-of-a-kind pieces from quality glass beads, pearls, crystals, turquoise, coral, jade and rare stones at great prices. Even the do-it-yourselfers, whether beginning beaders or seasoned stringers, can fashion simple strands of beads or dramatic multi-faceted, multi-strand beads all under Jenny's guidance.

Jenny admits that she grew up as a rough and tumble tomboy in the small town of Beeville, Texas, but she was attracted to jewelry design even as a young child. (Her mother encouraged her to string rocks instead of throwing them!) Even while she was in high school her friends began paying her to make their jewelry for proms and other special occasions. Soon, women began bringing their party and special event dresses to her so that she could work her magic with brilliant beads. Jenny is a true artist who loves mixing large, bold stones with dainty rare beads. Her selection of stones is very impressive, and her ready-made creations are very unusual. A few of her favorite combinations include green Baltic amber with ten-thousand-year-old fossilized ivory walrus tusk; blue London topaz with freshwater pearls, crystals and sterling silver; natural orange spiney oyster and gold vermeil, bronze freshwater coin pearls and Swarovski crystals. And, some of her most striking pieces are the multi-stranded freshwater pearls that are strung with beautiful turquoise.

Get individual attention and guidance in creating something original, or plan a group class for friends. Jenny also offers wholesale stones from all over the world to jewelers (who really wish they could keep her a secret!)

Jenny Forks is fast becoming a rare "gem" herself as she takes the jewelry world by storm, gaining national attention for her remarkable designs and workmanship. She is definitely a bright new face with a brilliant future. Treat yourself to a visit to this wonderful bead shop and learn the art of beading. For information on hours or classes call 210-558-0559 or visit www.bittercreekdesigns.com.

Knitting, Needlework & Stitchery

Yarnivore

You are probably asking, "What is a Yarnivore?" Owner Melanie Smith says, "Once a person begins to work with yarn, they consume it like a hungry animal!" Yarnivore, 2325 NW Military Hwy., is one of only a few specialty yarn and fiber stores in San Antonio. An avid knitter herself, Melanie realized the need for a store where knitters and spinners could find a large selection of high-quality yarn and fibers. She carries traditional wool and mohair yarns, as well as cotton, linen, ribbon and silk fibers. Before opening her shop, Melanie had a career as an environmental engineer, so she brings a unique perspective to her clients. This is evident by the rare yarns that she also carries, yarns made from soy, bamboo and corn. Customers will love the friendly atmosphere and comfy couches where they can KIP (Knit in Public). Classes are offered for beginning and advance knitters and spinners. Visit www.yarnivoresa.com or call 210-979-8255.

Restaurants & Coffee Houses

THE **LIGHTHOUSE**

You may already know that coffee can be refreshing to your body, but what about your spirit? At The Lighthouse Coffee & Café, 18730 Stone Oak Pkwy., and The Lighthouse at Olmos Park, 4212 McCullough Ave., mother-daughter owners Martha Garriffa and Lamae Koogler have created a slice of heaven right in San Antonio. These coffee shops and cafés offer an array of delicious coffees (and teas!) in a peaceful Christian atmosphere. In addition to great coffee, they offer a full menu. The Lighthouses' Chef, Eric Rocha, is a graduate of The Culinary Institute of America, Hyde Park, NY. Friday and Saturday evenings are extra special as local Christian musicians treat guests to live music at the Stone Oak location. Martha and Lamae also carry a wonderful selection of inspirational gifts and collectibles, like Demdaco's Willow Tree Angels. For more information, call 210-495-5099 the Stone Oak location or visit www.lhcafe.com.

The tall wood-beamed ceiling, huge arches and polished Saltillo tile floors (courtesy of well-known architects O'Neil Ford, Peter Callins and Cy Wagner) provide an authentic, romantic atmosphere for one of San Antonio's favorite upscale Mexican restaurants. The origin of La Fonda Oakhills, 350 Northhaven Dr., goes back three generations to the 1920s. Virginia Berry and her sister, Aunt Nanny, learned the art of preparing Mexican dishes in pre-revolutionary Monterrey, Mexico, where their father was a mining engineer. When they returned to San Antonio in 1929 they started a small toasted tortilla take-out service, selling tostados and hot sauce, which eventually grew into several great restaurants.

That same famous hot sauce, as well as all of the sisters' original recipes, are still served today at La Fonda Oakhills. Here in San Antonio, a Mexican restaurant is judged (quite critically) by its "chips and hot sauce," and La Fonda's is always rated top notch.

Owned by Virginia's grandson John Berry, La Fonda has retained the authenticity of John's grandmother's special dishes. He has expanded the menu to include Mexican seafood, steaks and great Southwestern cuisine. From the soft, handmade corn and flour tortillas to the creamy pralines, the entire meal is absolutely delicious. Add one of La Fonda's famous hand-squeezed Margaritas, and you have the perfect Mexican dinner.

There are private party rooms for special events, and La Fonda also offers catering services for off-site functions. For more information, visit www.lafondaoakhills.com. or call 210-342-8981.

It's an oasis in the heart of San Antonio. Los Patios is a 20-acre sanctuary, at 2015 NE Loop 410, that offers delicious food and fun shopping in a natural, preserved environment. Nomadic Indians once inhabited Los Patios' grounds. They were as drawn to the lush landscape as you'll be. In 1968, a Midland, Texas, oilman opened Los Patios. In 1999, he sold it to his long-time employees Russell and Diana Flores, and business associate John McClung and John's wife Mary. The new owners continue to offer delicious food in the enchanting setting. The signature dishes, like The Gazebo Combination and Chilaquiles, are delectable, and the Sunday brunch is a real treat. You'll also love visiting the property's boutiques, which specialize in clothing, jewelry, fine art and leather. There's even a florist, salon and photographer, convenient for onsite weddings and parties. Call 210-655-6171 or visit www.lospatios.com.

Salons, Spas & Indulgence

The New Images

Voted one of the top ten salons in San Antonio by *Travel Magazine*, this beautiful salon continues to garner raves from customers for its excellence. The New Images, 2191 NW Military Hwy., is located in Castle Hills Township, one of San Antonio's most exclusive, upscale shopping areas.

Owner Sharon Grimes purchased the salon from a previous owner, and has, with the help of a devoted husband and loyal customers, tripled the floor space and personnel, making it a full-service hair salon. The New Images can help you with any of your pampering needs—haircuts, styles, manicures, pedicures, facials, waxes and massage. It is also the perfect place to find unusual gifts and fashion accessories, including beautiful jewelry. Ask to see the handmade rhinestone Havaianas. Call 210-366-0651 for more information or to schedule an appointment.

Hair • Nails • Skin • Photo Styling

As distinctive as its reputation, K Charles & Co.'s great hair design is unparalleled. Seen in *Marie Claire, Harper's Bazaar, Elle, Glamour, Mademoiselle* and *Salon Today*, it is clear that the styling talent offered at K Charles & Co. salons is unmatched. Accolades continue for one of San Antonio's most respected, upscale salons.

Third generation hair and photo stylist, Kathy Thalman opened the first K Charles salon in 1984 and pioneered incredible changes in the industry by bringing the Aveda Institute to San Antonio. The beautiful salon at 18720 Stone Oak Pkwy. was one of the first businesses to open in the Stone Oak area, and is one of three K Charles salons in the city today. The K Charles professionals are experts in cut, style and color. They can help you with everything from simple, everyday cuts to sophisticated, glamorous styles.

The Aveda Institute is housed in part of the historic Pearl Brewery at 312 Pearl Pkwy. It was founded to educate students in hair, skin, makeup and nail care, as well as to instill in them the importance of total body wellness. Aveda's products are pure flower and plant essences and plant-based products. The Institute prepares graduates for state licensing examinations and careers in the beauty industry. For more information about the Aveda Institute, call 210-222-0023 or visit www.avedaisa.com.

Kathy's commitment to excellence and foresight in opening K Charles salons and San Antonio's Aveda Institute makes it easy to see why K Charles & Co. is one of the area's most respected, upscale salons and one of the fastest growing salon chains in the country. For more information and other locations, visit www.kcharlesco.com or call 210-403-0955.

Specialty Shops

When Jane Davis-Toerner "moved south" from Boston in 2001, she says, "It felt like I had moved to Mars! Even the birding seasons were backwards." It didn't take long though for her to fall in love with the friendly folks of San Antonio, or for her to find the perfect place for her charming store in Bracken Village. The Curious Naturalist, 18771 Nacogdoches Rd., is a diverse collection of birdhouses, feeders and baths for the backyard, and a wonderful selection of unique gifts for nature lovers. Jane has an extensive background as a birder and naturalist. She has worked at two different bird sanctuaries and taught many children's programs. Her knowledge and enthusiasm for birding is contagious, and part of the reason The Curious Naturalist has become a favorite place to shop and learn. We loved the window hummingbird feeders that bring those fascinating tiny birds up close for an exciting birding experience. Visit www.curiousnaturalist.com or call 210-651-0446.

The minute you walk through the door of Homestead Handcrafts you'll know you have found a store that will soon become a favorite. You will find everything from primitives and handmade furniture to Shabby Chic and collectibles. Owner Lisa Neubauer has been in the arts and crafts business for more than 20 years, and loves the antique and interior design business. She keeps everything exciting with annual Easter egg hunts, Christmas cookie contests and great sidewalk sales. Share the laughter and fun between the customers, owner and 200 vendors as you browse the incredible variety of merchandise. Stop by either location for double the fun, 4536 Thousand Oaks Dr. and 21518 Blanco Rd. in San Antonio. Visit www.homesteadhandcrafts.com or call 210-637-1842, 210-402-1221.

Wines

Bootlegger's Fine Wine & Spirits

Will and Cassie Lynch have been in the liquor and wine industry for more than 19 years, but Will's family's experience dates back to the 1930s. His knowledge of the business and their combined commitment to excellent customer service has made their store a long-time San Antonio success. Bootlegger's Fine Wines & Spirits, 8055 West Ave., is a beautifully decorated store that succeeds in being inviting to both women and men. The Lynches are hands-on in helping customers with wine selections, and offer wine tasting to ensure satisfaction. They carry boutique and low volume wines as well as high-end spirits like single malt Scotch and small batch Bourbons. You can also choose from an assortment of fine European chocolates, which are all natural and/or organic. Great store—extremely friendly staff! Call 210-348-8833.

Discover Bandera

Real cowpokes, cattle drives and country music; branding irons, bluebonnets and pit smoked BBQ; guitars, golf and good times—that's Bandera, "The Cowboy Capital of the World!" Sitting in just about the prettiest part of the Texas Hill Country, amid lush rolling hills and spring-fed creeks, the laid-back friendly town of Bandera, says, "Howdy" in true Western style.

Bandera is a small town that has somehow retained the authentic flavor of the Old West. You'll see it in the smiles of the townspeople as they tip their cowboy hats. You'll taste it in the mouthwatering barbecue and chuck wagon fare, and you'll experience it through the area's many exciting and unique activities and celebrations. From rodeos, trail rides and cattle drives to cowboy storytellers and Texas "two-steppin," you will enjoy a true bit of the Old West in this charming Hill Country town.

Early Bandera

Bandera's rich heritage and history dates back to the early 1700s when skirmishes between the Native Americans and the Spanish were predominate in the area. Historical lore says that the pass for which the town was named was the dividing line between the two territories, and a flag or "bandera" in Spanish, was placed at the highest point in the pass as a marker. Many battles ensued, and the Texas Rangers appeared in the area in 1841. But it wasn't until about 1851 that the first settlers began to make their way to the banks of the Medina River and the "Bandera" pass.

The settlement of Bandera was officially founded in 1853 as

a cypress shingle camp. The early residents harvested the cypress trees along the banks of the Medina and processed them into shingles. This small industry attracted many settlers, and in 1854 a Mormon colony was established. Bandera's first Polish settlers arrived in 1855. The town today remains one of the oldest Polish communities in the United States, and St. Stanislaus Catholic Church is the second oldest Polish church in the United States.

After World War I Bandera's economy was dependant mostly on cattle ranching, and the county was a staging area for cattle drives up the Western Trail. Sheep, however, were easier to raise and soon outnumbered cattle as the main source of income. During the 1920s the tourist trade began to take a front seat in Bandera's economy when local ranchers began to open their ranches to summer boarders and "dude ranches" became a popular option for family vacations.

Bandera Today

The pioneering spirit of the first settlers has lived on through their descendants, who found ways to survive and prosper in this rugged hill country. Today, it is still a small town of hard-working, hard-playing townsfolk—a collection of ranches and dude ranches with a rustic Main Street, a bar district, and lots of great country music venues. The town was once the gathering place for six million head of longhorn cattle that traveled the famed Western Trail. Visitors today will still see trail rides and cowboys on horseback and can attend a real rodeo or horse show. Not much has changed through the years in Bandera, and that's just how the locals like it. They invite visitors to "live it up, and slow it down," in one of the most breathtaking areas of the Texas Hill Country.

There is so much to do and see in Bandera, you'll want to take your boots off and stay awhile! The town revels in its Western heritage with celebrations and events every month of the year. Every Saturday April through December "Cowboys on Main," feature a real cowboy display such as chuck wagons and trick ropers on horses all in front of the courthouse, as well as strolling musicians on Main Street. The event is sponsored by the Frontier Times Museum Living History Project, a great place to learn about Bandera's early history.

At the Museum you will see more than 40,000 items of frontier relics, including a mounted Gila monster, a real shrunken head, a copy of the Bandera Bugle (the first local newspaper), Western art and artifacts, showcases of pictures and items from early pioneer days, and even bottles from Judge Roy Bean's saloon.

Cowboys and Honky Tonks

It's a fact that in Bandera you'll see cowboys on every corner. And, these ain't drugstore cowboys either! Bandera boasts the largest per capita number of world rodeo champion cowboys, and the town has a monument to prove it. The late artist Norma Jean Anderwald designed the monument on the courthouse lawn, which is dedicated to seven cowboy champions from Bandera County. You'll see cowboys in their high gear and Western gear and at local rodeos held each Tuesday and Friday night through the summer at the Twin Elm Guest Ranch.

They might be called nightclubs in the fancy city, but in Bandera, they're known as honky tonks, where country music reigns as king. The town is beloved for its musical heritage and has been called a "cradle of Texas music." *Texas Monthly* calls the town one of the state's top music destinations. The town is alive with great music in the saloons and cowboy bars on Main Street Wednesday through Sunday and its musical history is documented in the Bandera Music Hall of Fame. You can boot scoot on sawdust-covered floors till the cows come home.

Saddle Up for Fun

Of course, everyone knows that Bandera is touted as "The Cowboy Capital of the World," but it also proclaims itself to be the "Dude Ranch Capital of the World." Tourists can experience first hand what it means to be a real cowboy in Bandera because Dude Ranches abound throughout the county.

What is a "dude ranch?" It is a resort patterned after a real Western ranch, and is many times a real working ranch. If you are looking for a unique experience for the entire family, a visit to a Bandera dude ranch will be one remembered for a lifetime. Many feature horseback riding, camping (and campfires), outdoor sports, hayrides, Western bands, trick ropers, chuck wagon meals and, of course, Texas BBQ. You will enjoy the fresh Hill Country air, lots of wide-open spaces, the chill of a running spring, the warmth of the setting sun, and maybe even the delight of sleeping under the beautiful Texas stars. Some offer fishing, swimming, tennis and championship golf. You will read in the following pages of our book about the Flying L Guest Ranch and the Silver Spur Guest Ranch, two authentic and fun "homes on the range," sure to please every member of the family.

A Lady's Day Out in Bandera

This town full of cowboys, dude ranches and country music is truly a place where everything you've heard about Texas still exists. In fact the locals say that in Bandera, the "Fun Never Sets!" You can dig into a delicious apple pie or jar of homemade jelly, sport a silver belt buckle, listen to a tall tale, two-step with your honey, hunt for fossils, catch a dragonfly, pick a pumpkin, or put a quarter in a jukebox and listen to a classic country artist. A short (and beautiful) drive lands you in Lost Maples State Natural Area, a birder's paradise known for its breathtaking fall foliage. The 5,500-acre Medina Lake offers fishing, swimming, boating and camping for outdoor lovers. Also, wonderful lodging opportunities throughout the county offer guests a chance to enjoy the beauty of the great Texas Hill Country.

We've saved the best for last—great shopping! From unique Native American jewelry and primitive antiques to Texas crafts and homemade furniture, shopping Bandera will keep you busy for days. A charming "general store" sports Texas souvenirs and an old-timey soda fountain is available when you're ready for a sweet treat.

Pull on your cowboy boots, grab your cowboy hat and tie on a Western bandana for your visit to one of Texas' most unique and charming towns.

For additional information about Bandera, contact the Bandera Convention & Visitors Bureau at www.banderacowboycapital.com, 830-796-3045 or 800-364-3833. Or, contact the Bandera County Texas Chamber of Commerce at 830-796-3280, or visit www.banderatex.com.

Bandera Fairs Festivals & Fun

January
Bandera County Junior Livestock Show & Rodeo
Cowboy Capital Trail Ride

February
Cowboy Mardi Gras

March
Chili Cook Off
Fish Fry
Wild Hog Explosion

April
Cowboys on Main (April - Dec)
Spring Fling
Thunder in the Hill Country

May
Arts & Crafts Fair
Cowboys on Main (April - Dec)
Cowboy Capital Pro Rodeo
Medina Lake BBQ Cook Off
Spring HC-SNAP Trail Ride

June
Cowboys on Main (April - Dec)
River Fest

July
Cowboys on Main (April - Dec)
4th of July Parade & BBQ
Artifacts Art Show
National Day of the American Cowboy

August
Cowboys on Main (April - Dec)

September
Cowboys on Main (April - Dec)
Brisket Cook Off
Cajun Festival and Gumbo Cook Off
Celebrate Bandera
Rumble on the River

October
Cowboys on Main (April - Dec)
Great Hill Country Pumpkin Patch
Ranch Heritage Weekend
Quilt Show

November
Cowboys on Main (April - Dec)
Harvest Fest
Hunters Bar-B-Que and Outdoor Expo

December
Cowboys on Main (April - Dec)
Christmas in Hill Country
Holiday Parade

BANDERA COUNTY CVB

Where else could you see a real cattle drive, judge the best Texas chili, catch a wild hog or enjoy a true Western rodeo? Bandera, known as the "Cowboy Capital of the World," packs quite a lot of exciting Western entertainment into its quaint downtown and beautiful hill country. From bluebonnets and barbecue to chuck wagons and country music, the fun never ends in this unique Texas town. It is home to the best dude ranches in the country, and a place where visitors can take advantage of the weekly rodeos from May to September, the Frontier Times Museum, and exciting festivals that offer something for every age. Every month of the year is filled with fun, music, history, food, festivals, and of course, lots of "cowboys!" For more information on entertainment opportunities, contact the Bandera County Convention and Visitors Bureau at 830-796-3045, 800-364-3833 or visit www.banderacowboycapital.com.

Antiques & Interiors

Artifacts, 714 Main St. in Bandera, is filled with fabulous pieces from Europe, China and India. "This is not a cowboy store," explains owner Arthur Crawford, and he describes Artifacts' specialties as "architectural pieces" and "country-store items." You'll find antique iceboxes, glass-fronted hardware cabinets and advertising signs. Architectural pieces include doors, stained-glass windows, columns and arches. Many of these are crafted from teak and have a very primitive feel. From the European peddler's wagon and row of old wooden school desks to the stacked antique suitcases and ventriloquists' dummies, the store's ambiance is truly unique to this part of Texas. For more information, visit www.artifactsofbandera.com or call 830-796-9669.

Housed in one of the oldest and largest historic buildings in Bandera, The Love's Antiques Mall of Bandera, 310 Main St., is a fascinating place to shop. Owners Randy and Pamela Love opened this incredible antique haven in 1998 when they returned to the Texas Hill Country they loved and missed.

With more than 100 vendors in over 20,000 square feet, there is truly something for everyone. We found exquisite vintage and broken china jewelry, Esther Benedict iron sculptures, beautiful art, period antiques from around the world and unique Western memorabilia. Call 830-796-3838 for more information.

Artists, Art Galleries & Furniture

Esther Benedict Sculptures

Famed sculptor Esther Benedict knew from an early age that her career would involve either her love of horses or her love of art. Fortunately by combining both, she has become one of the most widely acclaimed metal artists today. Born and raised in New York State, Esther attended the State University of New York at Delhi, earning a degree in Horse Management. She then graduated from the Oklahoma State Horseshoeing School in Ardmore and became a farrier. Over the next few years she earned her AFA Journeyman's certification, the highest level you could earn at that time. After shoeing horses for more than 16 years, Esther decided to pursue her other love—art. Using her farrier's knowledge of metals and welding, Esther began to sculpt horses, capturing their strength and character with different textures and shapes. Today, her work is exhibited across the country. Her subjects range from horses and wildlife to human figures. Esther uses a signature technique to bring cold metal to life, and draws upon her knowledge and love of animals to sculpt pieces that are detailed with the "essence of life."

And her latest endeavor is life-size bronze sculptures. A few years ago, Esther fell in love with this form of sculpting when she was commissioned to create three life-size children by Fountain Technologies in Chicago. These pieces were of the Mississippi River era and are on display at Bass Street Landing in Moline, IL.

You can select a sculpture from what Esther might have in her current collection or have a sculpture custom made. Esther works from drawings or photographs, and creates each piece by hand.

Esther Benedict is a true sculptor. No matter what your style, you'll find something that you love. For more information, call 830-460-8176 or visit www.estherbenedict.com. The studio is located at 2225 Hwy. 16 S. in Bandera. By appointment only.

TEXAS COUNTRY FURNITURE

Scott Gambell's first woodworking experience was with his grandfather when he was very young, creating toy boats and guns from wood. Although he says that his mother wanted him to be President of the United States, he stuck with woodworking! Today Scott uses mesquite and cedar to craft fine custom furniture that looks as natural in ranch homes as it does in city dwellings. He describes his furniture as "elegant Western—built to last for generations." Texas Country Furniture, 5374 Hwy. 16 S. (halfway between Bandera and Pipe Creek), is a wonderful showroom of unique, handmade furniture, built to the highest standards of craftsmanship. You will find bedroom furniture, tables and chairs, cabinets, bar stools, rockers, outdoor furniture, and much more built from these woods. Scott also fills custom orders. Just send him a detailed drawing with dimensions and he will give you an estimate on a custom-made piece of fine "Texas Country Furniture." For more information, call 830-796-3311, 866-796-3311 or visit www.ranchdressin.com.

Cabins, Cottages, Guest Ranches & Golf

Hayrides, horseback rides and sing-a-longs around the campfire. A visit to the Flying L Guest Ranch at 566 Flying L Dr. in Bandera is a wagonload of fun for the entire family. This incredible Western guest ranch rambles across 772 acres of beautiful Texas Hill Country, and is the perfect place for families to stay and play together. You will make memories that will last a lifetime!

All of the Flying L rooms are suite-style villas, and can accommodate from four to six guests. Award-winning country breakfasts are served buffet style in the main house each morning. You will also enjoy the Creekside Cowboy Cookout, which gives you the option of eating your dinner "under the stars."

Put on your hat and pull on your boots for an early morning hayride to the stables, where you can take a guided horseback ride through the rolling hill country. If golf is more your cup of "tee," the par 72, 18-hole golf course offers challenging play. You can stay busy every minute of the day playing volleyball, basketball or tennis, swimming, hiking or fishing. Or you may prefer to sleep till noon and just enjoy the breathtaking beauty and serenity of the ranch. Kids absolutely love the Children's Activities Program, which includes nature hikes, horse clinics, hayrides, crafts and scavenger hunts. There is also a wonderful General Store, which features unique gifts, jewelry, and items from all over the world. Nights at the Flying L are as unforgettable as the action-packed days. There is Western entertainment and marshmallow roasts around a roaring campfire every night, or you may stumble across some good ole Western gunslingin 'and ropin'. However you choose to spend your days here, they will be memorable, filled with all the wonder and tranquility the Hill Country has to offer. For information, call 830-460-3001, 800-292-5134 or visit www.flyingl.com.

Trade in your power suit for blue jeans and your tie for a red bandana. Then head to the Silver Spur Guest Ranch in Bandera for a weekend you will never forget! This beautiful, historic ranch, located at 9266 Bandera Creek Rd., is owned and operated by Garry and Kay Walsmith and their family. It is the perfect place for families to enjoy a real Western experience in some of Texas's most beautiful Hill Country.

The rustic lodge includes spacious guest rooms, a cozy fireplace, player piano, billiard and ping-pong tables, and rocking chairs on the front porch that are perfect for "settin" and watching the incredible Western sunsets. Three hearty meals are served each day in the dining room, and baked goods, snacks and beverages are available all day. You'll be able to get your ten-gallon hat and choose your mount for a two-hour horseback ride on a guided trail, or spend the day lazing by the junior Olympic pool. In the evening, get ready for exciting Western entertainment, hayrides, campfires and melt-in-your-mouth s'mores.

The Silver Spur Guest Ranch is also the perfect place for any special event. The staff can accommodate large family reunions, church retreats, youth groups, corporate meetings and tour groups. The Ranch is also a popular place for weddings and receptions. You can plan a ceremony under the shaded trees or even on horseback, and a formal reception for as many as 200.

For one of the most memorable occasions in your life, plan your visit to this premier Texas dude ranch. Day visitor rates are available as well, and include a hearty wrangler breakfast or lunch, horseback riding, swimming, hiking and lots of friendly cowboy hospitality. For information, call 830-796-3037 or visit www.silverspur-ranch.com.

MEDINA RIVER GUEST COTTAGE
BANDERA CREEK GUEST HOUSE
BANDERA CREEK GUEST COTTAGE

Imagine retreating to a cozy rock cottage secluded on 27 beautiful Hill Country acres, enjoying the breeze from a screened porch or strolling to the crystal clear, spring-fed river just down the hill. The Medina River Guest Cottage, 871 Benton Creek Rd. (just outside Medina,) is just one of many spectacular rental properties offered by Guilott Realty, Inc. Overlooking the Medina River, this tucked-away cottage features exposed rock interior walls, a large rock fireplace and vaulted ceilings. The bedroom has a king-sized bed and sitting area, and the sumptuous bath has an antique pedestal sink and claw-foot tub. Peaceful, serene and romantic are words guests have used to describe their experiences at this wonderful river guesthouse.

Owner Gay Guilott also offers other country rentals, including the Bandera Creek Guest House, 141 W. Robindale Rd. in Bandera. This handsomely restored home overlooks Bandera Creek, and features Western décor. (Bandera is, after all, the Cowboy Capital of the Country!)

Just down the road you'll find another perfect escape—the Bandera Creek Guest Cottage, 148 W. Robindale Rd. Here, ancient oaks shade a wonderfully landscaped yard, and the cypress-lined Bandera Creek provides hours of serene contemplation.

All of these spectacular properties offer a peaceful, private retreat in a rustic, Hill Country setting, yet all have modern amenities. For more information, call 830-460-3517, 800-796-7757 or tour each cottage at www.ggrealty.com. (*See related story page 93.*)

Fashion & Accessories

BACK IN THE SADDLE
Unique Boutique

Back in the Saddle is a cowgirl's paradise! Looking for that perfect gift for your stylish girlfriend or yourself? Look no further than 1107 Cedar St. in Bandera because at this boutique, you'll find cowgirl-chic clothing, jewelry, gifts and accessories, plus an entire children's room. Its motto is "Your friend in fashion," and Back in the Saddle is sure to become one of your best friends once you visit!

Fashionable on-site owner, Lou Miller, looks forward to meeting you in person and helping you find that perfect item. Call 830-796-3911.

SHOE BIZ

More than just an ordinary shoe store, Shoe Biz is an attractively appointed shop filled with wonderful accessories like jewelry, lingerie, and of course, fabulous shoes! Shoe Biz is owned by Peggy Ashmore and daughter, Robin Gooding, so it is filled with laughter, love and family. You will find lines of sportswear by Christine Alexander, great tees and jackets with Swarovski crystals and respected brands of shoes such as Clarks of England. Shoe Biz is located at 301 Main St. within the historic Huffmeyer Building, the oldest commercial building in Bandera. For more information, call 830-796-8302.

Gifts, Home Décor, Florists & Soda Fountains

The Gingerbread House

The inviting window dressing gives you just a taste of the treasures you will find inside The Gingerbread House, 1110 Cedar St., in Bandera. It is filled with wonderful gifts, stunning home décor and the fabulous aroma of fresh floral arrangements. You will love the collection of items from Precious Moments, Hallmark and Sweetshop Candy. And, you won't want to miss Margaret Paradee's floral designs, which have made her shop a favorite for weddings and special events since 1980. Margaret also owns Bandera Wedding Planner, a professional service that will make your special day stress free. For more information, call 830-796-3616, visit www.thegingerbreadhouseflorist.com or www.banderaweddingplanner.com.

FRONTIER
outfitters★com

When Alexa Robinson started her e-commerce business back in 1997, the directions to her office read, "Cross two cattle guards and take your first right." This led to an old building everyone called "Trigger," where Alexa sold works from Texas Hill Country artisans and regional leather goods online. "I had to sell three of my longhorn cattle to purchase my first computer," she says. "Shipping and processing orders were all done from a shed with an extension cord for a power source!"

Alexa continues to "outfit the new frontier" with Frontier Outfitters. She has expanded her Internet business to include the retail store, an interactive online bridal registry, as well as a mail order catalog business while continuing with the same unprecedented service and reputation. Frontier Outfitters is now located in the historic Hatfield Building, which was built from Texas caliche limestone in 1888. Everyone that visits this remarkable store is amazed at the wonderful collection of Western home furnishings and décor, gifts, jewelry, and leather products by Montana Silversmiths and Double D Ranch. Alexa also showcases unusual pieces from local artists, as well as vendors from Washington to Florida.

Frontier Outfitters online bridal registry is easy to use, allowing couples to browse more than 1,000 products and register for gifts of their choice. They can design a Western bedroom, set a rustic teak table with fabulous dinnerware collections, or just add a Western touch with spectacular glassware and rustic table linens. (The delicious chocolate tamales make great wedding favors!)

Don't miss this incredible store, on Medina's Main Street at 13937 State Hwy. 16 N. For more information, visit www.frontieroutfitters.com or call 830-589-2926, 866-836-6880.

The Bandera General Store is housed in a 100-year old building at 306 Main St. The building has gracefully aged, retaining much of its original architecture, including beautiful high tin ceilings and original wood flooring. You can even see the row and seat numbers on the floor from its former days as the Bantex Theatre. Customers love perusing the antique step-back oak shelves filled with unique Western gifts, Texas jams, jellies and salsas; and kids can't wait to taste the old-fashioned, hard-to-find candies. The nostalgic soda fountain, complete with metal spinning stools, is a favorite gathering place for all ages to enjoy delicious banana splits, malts, Blue Bell Ice Cream, cherry Cokes and old-fashioned sodas. Don't be surprised if "Henry" the resident friendly ghost joins you for a treat. Owners Bob, Gail and Shelia Click, employees and customers have all been the target of Henry's mischievous pranks. For more information, call 830-796-4925.

Hotels & Inns

River Oak Inn and Restaurant

When it's time to get away from the bustle of city life, head to "cowboy country" for a weekend at one of Bandera's most peaceful inns. The River Oak Inn and Restaurant is located at 1203 Main St., right in the middle of the beautiful Texas Hill Country. Many of the rooms are country-style suites and the entire Inn offers visitors a "home-away-from-home" welcome. Dinner can be served inside the restaurant or on the porch, which overlooks the Medina River and the beautiful wooded oaks. Enjoy the tranquility of a Koi pond, waterfalls, or drive a short distance to Garner State Park or Lost Maples. For more information, call 830-796-7751.

Realtors

Your Real Estate Professionals
Established 1981

Offering premier properties like ranches, homes, waterfront acreage and rentals, Guilott Realty, Inc.'s friendly team of professionals has a thorough knowledge of the beautiful Texas Hill Country. Owner and Bandera resident Gay Guilott opened her company in 1981, and loves serving the community with her professional expertise and personal involvement in numerous charities and civic events. Stop by 129 State Hwy. 16 S., visit www.ggrealty.com or call 830-460-3517 or 800-796-7757. *(See related story page 87.)*

Salons, Spas & Indulgence

Spoiled Rotten Salon
and
Butter Beans Boutique

"Spoiled Rotten" is what you'll be after visiting this full-service salon and chic boutique. Located at 215 14th St. in Bandera, Spoiled Rotten Salon and Butter Beans Boutique can help you relax with a massage or create a new look. The talented and friendly staff will help you with everything from hair color to pedicures, jewelry to trendy fashions and more. A perfect stop for your Lady's Day Out pampered experience. Call 830-796-9446 for an appointment or just stop by.

Discover Boerne

Willkommen! Welcome to Boerne, one of the Texas Hill Country's most charming and historic towns. This charismatic town is filled with unusual history, fun atmosphere, great shopping, wonderful food and generous people who open their arms as wide as their smiles to every visitor. With its delightful and surprising mixture of Texas Hill Country beauty and deep-rooted German heritage, Boerne (pronounced "Bernie") is the perfect place for an unforgettable "Ladies Day Out!"

Newcomers to Boerne will delight in the seven-block Historic Main Street or "Hauptstrasse," filled with incredible shopping and dining opportunities. (We've covered it all for you!) The nationally acclaimed Cibolo Wilderness Trail offers the entire family fun-filled hours of nature exploration and easy hiking. The Agricultural Heritage Center is a must-see, with an exhibition of antique farm equipment and a working blacksmith shop. And, of course, the breathtaking Guadalupe River is just minutes away, offering visitors spectacular outdoor water adventure. Boerne is an amazing town that has held fast to the ancestral heritage of its early German settlers, welcoming all who visit to share in their love for this beautiful rolling hill country and sample both the food and traditions of their past.

Historic Boerne

The city of Boerne was named for the German poet and publicist Ludwig Borne who inspired many to leave Germany and settle here along the north side of Cibolo Creek in a settlement called Tusculum. After many of the first settlers moved on, the land was bought by Gustav Theissen and John James, who platted the town in 1852. It was at this time that the name was changed to honor Ludwig Borne. The Kendall County Courthouse was built in Boerne in 1870, and is still in use, making it the second oldest courthouse in Texas.

With the arrival of the San Antonio and Aransas Pass Railway in 1887, Boerne's population grew to almost 800, and the town voted to incorporate in 1909. Although the community continued to prosper, the Great Depression caused many residents to move to San Antonio, making Boerne a sleepy, rural town. Ironically, it was San Antonio's growth and expansion during the 1960s, with the completion of Interstate 10 that restored new life and growth to Boerne. The German culture dominated the community, and it has been, in part, that allegiance to its heritage that has made the celebrated town so fascinating and popular. You will see it in the distinctive architecture of the downtown buildings and experience it in the excitement of the annual festivals. The German heritage colors this entire region with its warmth and personality.

Stroll the Hauptstrasse

Many of Boerne's street signs are the first indication of its interesting German history. In fact, the Main Street sign says "Hauptstrasse," which means "Main Street." Everything is within walking distance, so wear comfortable shoes because there is so much to see and do. Park at one end of the town and have fun exploring each and every shop for a world of treasures—from antiques, home accessories and garden delights to clothing, jewelry and gifts. It gets a little hard to concentrate on shopping (if that's possible) because of the incredible aroma of delicious treats from the bakeries and country cafés. You might even have to take a break and treat yourself to a glass of beer or wine at the local brewery.

Art Blooms in Boerne

Wildflowers aren't the only thing blooming in this Texas Hill Country town. Art is in full bloom here. Perhaps it is the breathtaking scenery of the countryside that inspires so many artists to pick up their brushes, but whatever the reason, Boerne is flourishing as an art community. In fact there are two art groups in town (The Cibolo Arts Council and the Boerne Area Artists Association) that promote the arts—visual arts, music and theater. On any given weekend you will see painters and sculptors at work on their crafts, and you will find many of their pieces in the local gift shops and galleries.

There has been a huge influx in the cultural arts in Boerne, and many of these business owners have opted to group together on Main Street just south of the Cibolo Creek. This area has been designated as the River South Arts & Design District, or the River South District, and is dedicated to promoting active cultural, dining and shopping opportunities for the enhancement of the quality of life in Boerne. You can look forward to receptions and exhibitions in the stores and galleries, as well as more arts and music festivals.

Festival Fun!

As you can imagine, a town with this much colorful history and heritage is bound to want to celebrate! Boerne invites locals and visitors to gather for great food and music throughout every season with antique shows, parades, festivals and fireworks. One of our favorites is Berges Fest—a swirling, twirling festival each June that takes place under "bier tents" set up on the Main Plaza. Other wonderful family memories can be made at the Hill Country Christmas, the Kendall County Fair, Dickens on the Main, Boerne Market Days, and the Hill Country Antique Show. And have you ever been to a "Chuck Wagon Cook-Off?" Cooks from dozens of authentic antique chuck wagons compete with their chicken fried steak, potatoes, biscuits and peach cobbler!

If you are visiting Boerne during the summer months, be sure to attend one of the town's famous "Abendkonzerte Summer Evening Concerts," which are held every other Tuesday sometime during June, July and August. The Boerne Village Band fills the Main Plaza with the traditional Oompah music, and picnic baskets overflow with German treats and sweets. This band was established before the Civil War, and, outside of Germany, is the oldest continuously active German band in the world. These Abendkonzerte are remarkable and memorable.

Antiques in Them Thar Hills!

Antique seekers and lovers of all things old head to Boerne during the fall for the legendary, two-day Key to the Hills Antique Show held at the Kendall County Fairground. Pumpkins and Indian corn decorate the booths of vendors from as far away as Oklahoma, Arizona and Kansas. These vendors fill their booths with antiques and collectibles, rare books, pottery, art, jewelry and vintage clothing.

The Boerne Optimist Hill Country Antique Show & Sale is held during the spring at the Fairgrounds, and is another opportunity for antique lovers to find furniture, textiles, paintings and architectural elements.

Unusual "Nightlife" in The Old Tunnel

The night can be one of the most fascinating times to get out and explore one of Boerne's most exciting natural treasures— The Old Tunnel. The Old Tunnel Wildlife Management Area (OTWMA) includes the abandoned railroad tunnel (Lower Level,) which is home to more than three million Brazilian free-tailed bats and 3,000 Cave myotis. Visitors come from everywhere from May through October to view the spectacular nightly emergence of bats, and enjoy an educational program about the history and ecology of the nocturnal (and somewhat mysterious) mammals. The Upper Viewing area of the OTWMA and Nature Trails are open to the public year-round, seven days a week, providing activities such as hiking, bird watching, plant identification, astronomy, guided nature walks and educational exhibits. For more information about this incredible wildlife adventure or directions to the Old Tunnel contact the Texas Parks and Wildlife Department (830-990-2860.)

Boerne's Natural Beauty

Whether you are visiting Boerne for a day or decide to stay for a lifetime, you'll find blissful peace and contentment in its gentle rolling hills, fresh air, incredible vistas and abundant wildlife. Aside from its great shopping, Boerne's outdoor recreational opportunities abound along the banks of the beautiful Cibolo Creek, in the 1,900-acre Guadalupe State Park and in the carved beauty of the cool caverns throughout the area. Be sure to visit the "Cave Without a Name," and just try to come up with a better name to describe its beauty. Even the lodging choices in Boerne provide opportunities to enjoy the beauty of the area. Hunting and fishing ranches, river resorts and tucked away country bed and breakfasts allow visitors to enjoy all of the rugged natural beauty and charm of this small Texas town.

For more information about Boerne, contact the Boerne Convention & Visitors Bureau at 830-249-7277, 888-842-8080 or visit www.visitboerne.org. Or, contact the City of Boerne at 830-249-9511 or visit www.ci.boerne.tx.us.

Boerne Fairs Festivals & Fun

January
Boerne Market Days (Second weekend every month)

February
Hill Country Optimists Antique Show
St. Valentines Day Motor Cycle Massacre

March
Chuck Wagon Cook-Off and Heritage Gathering
St. Peter's Art Auction

April
Antique Tractor Show & Pull
Parade of Artists
Texas Corvette Assn's Open Car Show

May
Historic Homes Tour

June
Abendkonzerte Summer Evening Concerts
Adventure Fest
Berges Fest
Dodge Charger Meet

July
Abendkonzerte Summer Evening Concerts
July 4th Fireworks Show

August
Abendkonzerte Summer Evening Concerts

September
Kendall County Fair

October
Festival of Arts and Music
Key to the Hills Rod Run
Key to the Hills Antique Show

November
Dickens on Main

December
A Hill Country Christmas
Oma's Christmas Fair
Weihnachts Fest

No matter how many times you visit Boerne, you can't quite contain an audible "Ahhhh" the minute you turn onto Main St. Everything about this quaint, old-fashioned town charms visitors. Families are drawn to the Cibolo Creek, which runs through the middle of downtown, and to Boerne Lake for swimming, fishing, windsurfing or snorkeling. Every day of the year Main Street or "Hauptstrasse," is filled with wonderful dining and shopping opportunities, including antique stores, trendy boutiques, garden centers, jewelry and gift shops and of course incredible eateries.

Many of the businesses are located within historic stone buildings that were built during the mid to late 1800s, making shopping in Boerne a real treat. Be sure to save time for a walking tour of the Historical District, visiting places like The Historic Kendall County Courthouse and old jail; the Historic Boerne Cemetery, which dates to 1867 and includes the grave of George Wilkins Kendall; the Kuhlmann-King Historical House and Museum; and the Menger-Kingsbury-Shumard House, which houses the Boerne Convention & Visitors Bureau. Located at 1407 S. Main St., the Visitor Information Center is a great place to begin your tour. (This rock house is believed to date back to 1841—before the city of Boerne or Kendall County were even founded.)

Take your time to explore all of the celebrated and exciting adventures of this Hill Country treasure. Stay a day or two in a cozy bed and breakfast, sample treats from the local bakeries and have the time of your life at one of the many special events! For information about Boerne, call 830-249-7277, 830-249-8000 or visit www.visitboerne.org or www.boerne.org.

Antiques & Interiors

GOOD & CO.

With its cottage-chic environment, Good & Co. located at 248 S. Main St. in Boerne's historic district, is no "Ho-Hum Home" store. It is comprised of three buildings, including a historic 1858 structure—the oldest in Boerne—filled with wonderful English, French and Northern European antiques, upholstered pieces, reproductions and accessories. And you won't want to miss its great selection of lamps and wall art.

Suzy Romike originally opened Good & Co. in 1991 in the coastal city of Corpus Christi. She then traded the seaside locale for Houston—the energy capital—in 1993. Good & Co. thrived in a tree-shaded cottage on a busy thoroughfare in River Oaks, but in 1997, Suzy decided to trade the hustle and bustle of the big city for the historic ambiance of Boerne.

Now joined by family members Ronda Romike and Mike and Allison Romike, this transplanted South Texas family has put down new roots in the heart of the Texas Hill Country. These small town roots reaffirm the family's values of self-reliance and personal integrity. Each member of the family contributes their own special talent, and the Romike family's labor of love has turned into a hugely successful business.

Good & Co. continues to offer a dazzling selection of painted country furnishings, antiques, garden ornaments, fountains, architectural elements, and unusual finds that possess good lines, good design, and good patina.

The staff of Good & Co. strive to keep customers coming back for more. With constantly changing merchandise, Suzy, her family and staff will help you find just the treasure to cozy up your home. For more information, call 830-249-6101.

Artists & Art Galleries

Bill Zaner's Art Haus

Originally established in 1975 when owner and artist Bill Zaner moved to Boerne with his family, Bill Zaner's Art Haus, 255 S. Main St., will captivate you with its breathtaking exhibits by many notable Texas artists. From paintings to woodcarvings, sculpture to pottery, you'll meander through this gallery, which is now housed in a historic 1880s building, and be in awe of the talent displayed within.

Bill began painting and drawing as a small child and went on to study under the Dean of Arizona Artists, Hal Empie. Bill has been a professional painter of portraits and landscapes all of his adult life, and now he specializes in landscapes. Bill's work is in many private and corporate collections. It can be seen at the Art Haus and at www.billzanerpaintstexas.com. Bill is also a gifted writer, producing a column for the local paper and authoring three books, one of which is his Texas Sketchbook. For more information, call 830-249-1650.

BELLA *Creo*

FINE ART • FINE JEWELRY
original works in all media by american artists

After 25 years of traveling to every corner of the United States as working artists, Tami and Charles Kegley have settled down in their favorite place—the Texas Hill Country. As artists, they both love and respect the aesthetic beauty and serenity of the area and appreciate the creativity it inspires. Their art is represented in a number of significant public and private collections, including the Renwick Gallery of the Smithsonian and the Los Angeles County Museum of Art. With a desire to share their art and represent one-of-a-kind works by quality artists, they opened a beautiful gallery that overlooks the historic millpond on Cibolo Creek at 412 River Rd. in Boerne. Bella Creo, which translates to "beautiful I create" in Italian, is a magnificent collection of original works in all media by American artists.

The Kegley's art includes outstanding sculptural works and exceptional jewelry designs featuring unusual gems in high karat gold. The artists they represent work as individuals or in small studio collectives. All work is original in design and execution. The Kegleys also value each artist as a friend and compatriot. "It is more important than ever for each of us to make those human connections," they say. "Bringing art into your personal space engages the heart, mind and soul."

Both Tami and Charles are very involved in the local arts community with organizations such as the Boerne Area Artist Association and the Cibolo Arts Council. "Come play with us and get inspired. We invite you to take a bit of the very vibrant Boerne arts scene home with you!" For more information about Bella Creo, visit www.bellacreo.com or call 830-248-1919. *(Color photo featured in front section of book.)*

Attractions & Entertainment

With its beautiful rolling hills, lush pastures and sparkling lakes, the 86-acre Enchanted Springs Ranch, 242 Hwy. 46 W. just outside of Boerne, is one of the most remarkable places in the Texas Hill Country. Although you will see all the signs of a typical working ranch—Texas longhorns, horses and cowboys, you will also feel as though you have stepped back in time because Enchanted Springs Ranch is also a Western town right out of the 1800s. Owners and operators Steve and Vicki Schmidt, and Grant and Pam Jacobs have created a magical Western time warp with a passion to "Keep the Old West Alive." The town has been used as the setting for movies, videos, documentaries and commercials, and has had more than 50,000 visitors from more than 80 countries. Ride through the ranch among buffalo and exotic animals, tour the movie set and history exhibit, and get a souvenir from the trading post.  A two-story log house is a bed and breakfast, and the entire town can be rented for any type of special event including weddings and receptions. There is even a "honeymoon cabin!" Call 830-249-8222, 800-640-5917 or visit www.enchantedspringsranch.com, for more information.

Hunting, fishing, hiking, tubing, canoeing, picnicking and just plain 'ole R&R. If this sounds like heaven, it almost is—at least a Texas Hill Country version! Secluded, beautiful Joshua Creek Ranch rambles over 1,200 magnificent acres and offers some of the best fishing and hunting around. Spring-fed Joshua Creek merges with the Guadalupe River on the northern boundary of the Ranch.

Owners Ann and Joe Kercheville bought the ranch in 1986 and opened it to guests in 1990. Take a European-style pheasant shoot, fly fish for rainbow trout, or plan a turkey or deer hunt. The ranch is known to have some of the best wingshooting opportunities in Texas. This is also a wonderful place for the entire family. The Outdoor Youth Adventure Program is a great experience for children in the summer, but even mom will fall in love with nature here. Located at 132 Cravey Rd. just 10 miles north of Boerne and open year-round for lodging and dining. Call 830-537-5090 or visit www.joshuacreek.com, for more information.

One of the "deepest, darkest secrets in Texas" is a place too beautiful to be described in mere words. The Cave Without A Name was given the moniker by the winning entry from a local student in a contest held to name the cave in 1939. Located on 170 acres at 325 Kreutzberg Rd., just 11 miles north of Boerne, this spectacular natural wonder still defies visitors to describe its beauty. The standard tour covers six major "rooms" of sparkling, crystalline formations—renowned for its drapery and formations up to 30 feet tall. The constant 66-degree cave environment makes this a great experience any time of the year. At the end of the tour you'll find a crystal clear subterranean stream fed from the Guadalupe River. In fact, for a truly incredible adventure, ask about the Adventure Tours where you don a wetsuit (provided) and hike a mile upstream, ten stories underground! The gift shop features an eclectic collection of items from rock and mineral samples to jewelry. A guided tour through The Cave is an exciting and educational adventure for the entire family. For more information, call 830-537-4212, 888-TEX-CAVE (839-2283) or visit www.cavewithoutaname.com.

Children's

Celebrating classic childhood memories, Topsy Turvy is a whimsical children's shop that is situated next to its companion store Cielo. Topsy Turvy is located in Boerne at 346 S. Main St. in the Old Spanish Trail gas station. This historic building has been transformed into a delightful store filled with classic children's apparel and layette, heirloom-quality furniture and bedding, charming gifts, and the largest selection of retro pedal cars in South Texas. Puzzles and toys abound for both boys and girls, as well as colorful books to nourish the imagination. Touching keepsakes can be found in glass cases, which overflow with jewelry fashioned from Austrian crystals, pearls and precious metals. Nostalgic clocks can also add a lighthearted touch to any child's room. Topsy Turvy will leave you longing to indulge your childlike side with tender mementos for the little ones you hold dear. For more information, call 830-249-0677 or visit www.topsyturvyshop.com. *(See related story page 117.)*

Condominiums, Resorts, Rentals & Golf

Tapatio Springs Golf Resort & Conference Center offers a wide range of activities in a quiet atmosphere. Visitors will be "touched" by the natural beauty of the rolling hills and beautiful lakes. This stately, 2100-acre resort is located in a beautiful valley just four miles south of Boerne deep in the Texas Hill Country at 314 Blue Heron Blvd., and only 15 miles from San Antonio. Tapatio is the ideal spot for relaxing and enjoying the outdoors. Residents refer to it as "city close and country quiet." Accommodations include 40 condos and 112 hotels rooms, with six suites and 12 junior suites. The two-and-three-bedroom townhouses overlook the par-35 Ridge Nine course and have a full kitchen, fireplace and patio. Each hotel room has either a patio or balcony on which you can soak up the day's beauty or watch the deer at sunset. Tapatio Springs is the perfect place for a family vacation or business meeting. For information or reservations, call 800-973-8183 or visit www.tapatio.com. *(See related story on page 120.) (Color photo featured in front section of book.)*

Fashion & Accessories

celeste
clothing • gifts • accessories

Every person who walks into Celeste, 140 S. Main St., leaves as a "friend" and loyal customer. This outstanding specialty boutique, which offers everything from classic styles to the latest trends, has something for everyone. Whether you are young or simply young at heart, you will find a wonderful collection of clothing and accessories from top designers, and the friendly staff will help you pull together the perfect look.

The store itself is a statement of style and fun. Owner Celeste McCabe is no stranger to retail, and her expertise is evident throughout the 2,000-square-foot space. Celeste has owned several clothing stores including one in Corpus Christi and one in Chicago. When she finally came "home" to Texas, Boerne was lucky to have her open one of the town's most popular and successful stores. The building's pressed tin ceiling, which dates back to the early 1900s, adds nostalgia to the antiques and Shabby Chic displays scattered throughout the store. One of Celeste's most popular clothing lines is Neesh by D.A.R.—a vintage construction garment for "grown-up girls." You will also love "Flax," a collection of wonderful linens, generously sized and perfect for our Southern climate. Among other lines, you'll also find handbags by Tano, Leaders in Leather and Hobo; lingerie by Simple Pleasures; shoes by Bernardo; and a superb selection of designer accessory items that you won't find just anywhere.

Celeste and her experienced staff have a knack for keeping their fingers on the pulse of the latest fashion trends. You will absolutely love shopping in this remarkable store, where you will find the latest clothing styles and must-have accessories! For more information, call 830-249-9660.

Bedazzled
Jewelz & Bagz

Three generations of Kellye Harris' family make Bedazzled, 302 S. Main St., one of the most exciting places to shop in Boerne. Seven rooms are filled with fashion and fun, including affordable blouses, stunning jewelry (one room filled with pieces at wholesale) gorgeous handbags and glamorous accessories. You'll find Swarovski crystals adorning clothing and belts by many West Coast designers and one-of-a-kind pieces designed by Kellye herself. For more information, call 830-816-8889

Florists

The Flower Shop, 437 S. Main St., is an incredible mix of antiques and flowers. Owner Shirley Wilson has an extraordinary talent for combining unique elements with flowers to create one-of-a-kind arrangements. This Boerne store, which is always decorated for the seasons, has been featured in the national magazine, *Florists' Review* and has been named "Best Florist" in Kendall County since 1999. The flowers and decorative items are displayed in small vignettes throughout the store, and the combinations are stunning. Let the talented staff of The Flower Shop help you with all of your floral needs—fresh and permanent. For more information, call 830-816-2042 or 800-807-5280.

Furniture, Gifts & Home Décor

Embodying the colorful, feisty spirit of one of our most loved female Western heroes, Calamity Jane's Trading Company is a must-visit paradise for Hill Country shoppers. The historic Boerne building at 322 S. Main St. is the perfect setting for all of the unusual pieces of Hill Country furniture and decorative items inside. The minute you walk through the door you will be greeted in grand style. From the gleaming copper tables and Western art, to the colorful outdoor pottery and hand-carved mesquite furniture, you'll find an amazing collection of unique accessories for your home or ranch. Many of the pieces are one-of-a-kind creations from the heart and mountains of Mexico and as far away as India. The use of animal hides along with luxurious fabric in furniture adds an early Western ambiance to the store, whether it is on the backs of dining room chairs, ottomans or even throw pillows. You are sure to find never-before-seen home décor like beds made from old carved doors, ornately carved armoires and distinctive chandeliers. Browse the rooms of unique items that bring to mind another place in time with exotic accessories that tie the present with the rugged spirit of the Old Wild West.

It is very evident that owner Shawn Beach and the friendly staff of Calamity Jane's Trading Company absolutely love what they do, and they are most proud of their one-on-one personal attention to each customer. They will gladly go the extra mile for everyone who walks through the door, whether it is with custom orders, design services or just a helping hand to the car with a fabulous find! For more information, visit www.calamityjanestradingco.com or call 830-249-0081.

The
Rusty Bucket

Antiques • Home Accents • Art

The Rusty Bucket is family owned and located in the heart of downtown Boerne at 195 S. Main St. The award-winning home décor and gift store is filled with an exquisite eclectic collection of hand-selected furniture pieces and home embellishments. The wide selection of decorative accents is well suited for the lifestyle of this store's diverse clientele. The Rusty Bucket carries many exclusive dealers such as Lynn Haney Santa's, Intrada Roosters (imported from Italy), Tassel's by former *Southern Living* Cooking School Director. Stop in and enjoy the friendly customer service and let the owners and their staff help you find the right décor or that special gift for anyone. Call The Rusty Bucket at 830-249-2288 for more information. *(Color photo featured in front section of book.)*

Hollyhock
jewelry • home decor • gifts • accessories

Named for Doris Savage's precious first-born daughter Holly, this charming gift boutique is as sweet as its name. Hollyhock is located in the middle of downtown Boerne at 305 S. Main St., and is a wonderful store filled with great gifts at great prices. Doris carries Keepers of the Light and Green Leaf candles, which you will notice the moment you open the door. Pet owners will adore the pet collars, mats and bowls by Ganz, but will especially love the dog and cat collars designed by Doris herself. Customers enjoy browsing the cases of fun costume jewelry, but the handmade purses are always the biggest hit. Each is a one-of-a-kind creation by Doris, and she says, "I can't seem to make them fast enough. Some customers will buy several at a time." You just won't be able to pass up all the wonderful treasures at Hollyhock! For more information, call 830-249-1048.

DISCOVER BOERNE **113**

The Burlap Horse

Heirloom furnishings and lifestyle accessories best describe this award winning and nationally recognized treasure—The Burlap Horse. The store is filled with classic Texas style, hand-selected continental European antiques and reproductions, and home accessories that range from the ranch heritage of yesteryear to the trends of tomorrow.

Owner Melissa Haberstroh named the store after an old pull toy (a burlap horse) she found at an antique auction. Her shop is Boerne's only source for items like Match Italian pewter, Sweet Dreams Bedding and Caldrea's line of aromatherapeutic items. Melissa carries exquisite linens, charming baby and pet items, and wonderful hostess gifts. The Burlap Horse turns into a "holiday wonderland" the first week of October each year, but is quite the "social hub-bub" all year with monthly store events, parties, trunk shows and educational opportunities. Stop by 609 S. Main St. for hours of enjoyment. For more information, call 830-249-0204 or visit www.burlaphorse.com.

Viva Rouge

Viva Rouge, 424 S. Main St., is located in a beautiful 1902 Victorian-style house in downtown Boerne, and we promise that it will become one of your favorite places to shop for beautiful home décor and quality furnishings. Owners Cathy and Keith Farmer say that their niche is "quality handmade products that are exclusive to our store and our area." They feature an ongoing selection of designer and handcrafted furnishings, including one-of-a-kind items designed by them or other local craftsmen. The Farmers are famous for their specialty items like copper, zinc and stainless tables and counter tops, which they make to order. They also carry MacKenzie-Childs home furnishings, Sid Dickens memory plaques and Vera Bradley purses and accessories. We loved the beautiful glassware and pottery, candles, jewelry and tabletop accessories. For more information, call 830-249-9787 or visit www.viva-rouge.com.

Although owners René and Lise Perez hail from very different backgrounds (René is a New Braunfels-born Texan, Lise was born in Copenhagen, Denmark), their talents and strengths complement each other perfectly. The result is one of the most beautiful and successful lighting and interior décor showrooms in Texas. The Gallery of Lighting, 28611 IH-10 W., is filled with luminous light from hundreds of magnificent chandeliers and lamps in modern, Tuscan, French Country, Western and vintage styles. "We are more than a lighting store we carry many unique home décor items and people spend hours browsing," says Lise. "They love our homey vignettes and realistic use of lighting." René adds, "Our new outdoor living area is getting lots of attention from home owners. We carry decorative outdoor lighting and art to accessorize outdoor entertaining." For more information, call 830-755-5346 or visit www.thegalleryoflighting.com. *(Color photo featured in front section of book.)*

At the Chateaux of the Dominion 2007 Parade of Homes, guess who was awarded "Best Furnishings"? That's right; Catrina's at the Ranch, 31300 IH-10 W., is a favorite, and we're sure it'll soon be one of yours. With a motto of "If You Can Dream It, We Can Build It," Catrina's offers a classic collection of handmade Texas to Tuscan style furniture, rugs, pottery, wrought iron and gifts.

Owner Catrina Hoelke has been sketching and designing furniture for more than 30 years, and she is an avid supporter of other designers too. In fact, she personally knows just about every artist whose work is showcased in her store. If you love Western or hacienda-style furniture, Catrina's has everything you could need—from chandeliers and lamps made from animal horns to cowhide rugs and Western art. For more information, call 830-755-6355 or visit www.catrinasattheranch.com. *(Color photo featured in front section of book.)*

Life sure has changed for Tina Cappello. This stylish, petite woman used to show longhorn cattle for a ranch in Bandera. That's a long way from her life as the owner of The Alley on Main, an eclectic gift shop and fashionable home décor boutique. The Alley on Main is smack dab in the middle of Boerne's downtown. Of course, this wasn't always the case. The shop got its name because it was initially an alley (yes, literally an alley!) between Boerne's Main Street and the alley behind the shops on Main Street. It has since moved to its present location at 152-A S. Main St., making it a welcome site in Boerne's delightful downtown area.

Tina goes out of her way to offer a variety of home décor accessories—from the traditional to the unusual. She also carries rustic furniture from Mexico, Votivo and Archipelago candles, and one-of-a-kind lamps. Tina is committed to serving her customers with a smile. She and her staff work with you to solve any of your decorating dilemmas, regardless of your home's interior theme. So whether you're looking to add that perfect little something to complete your room's look or starting from scratch, Tina and her friendly staff are there to assist you.

And if you're on the hunt for something stylish to wear, The Alley on Main has just what you need. In addition to beautiful pieces for the home, Tina brings her customers wonderful fashions and stunning accessories that are unique—and even better they won't break the bank.

For more information about The Alley on Main, call 830-249-3339.

 Cielo, which means "heaven" in the romance languages, is a luxurious shop located at 336 S. Main St. in Boerne's beautiful and historic Staffel building. Situated right next door to its companion children's shop, Topsy Turvy, Cielo specializes in unique indulgences for the bed and bath. European soaps, French jewelry, iron beds, decorative accessories and loungewear are just a few of the alluring items that await you. Luxury bed linens by Bella Notte and Pine Cone Hill are available to transform your bedroom into an ethereal retreat.

Owner Frank Treviño, a Houston transplant, has an extensive background in floral design—which includes designing for a former First Lady. Now specializing in dried flowers, this shop's state-of-the-art arrangements are not to be missed. Whether searching for a special gift for a dear friend or finding your own deliciously scented bath soap, Cielo is a treat for all the senses. For more information, call 830-249-9955. *(See related story page 107.)*

 Loyal customers have called this store a "treasure chest" since 1986. In fact, they voted it "Best Gift Shop in Boerne 2006." Lasting Impressions is located in the heart of historic downtown Boerne at 116 S. Main St. Plan to spend a good bit of time here because Lasting Impressions is filled floor to ceiling with so many wonderful gifts and treasures. You'll find great Texas Hill Country accents for the home—lamps, oak barrel furniture, tabletop accessories and decorative pieces. This is especially true from Thanksgiving to Christmas when the entire store gets dressed up for the Hill Country Christmas. Owner Barbara Peterson and her friendly staff invite you to browse the beautiful store for extraordinary gifts and stunning home décor. Call 830-249-4116 or visit www.ahillcountrychristmas.com for more information.

Jewelry

"Sculpture on a small scale" is what owner Jerry Gowen believes jewelry's true calling is...and he's spent a lifetime proving that to be true. His jewelry store, The Green Bull Jewelry Co. is located in the renovated 1898 Boerne Livery Stable and features many unusual and one-of-a-kind pieces.

At the age of six, Jerry made his first piece of jewelry, and in the years to follow, studied several art mediums, including oil painting and sculpture. After graduating from college with a degree in theology, Jerry continued to study jewelry technology at the Texas Jewelry Institute. Over the years, he has received numerous awards for his designs. His celebrated collection, "Simply Divine," features crosses in sterling silver, 18- and 22-karat gold, and colored gemstones and diamonds. And his Texas-inspired line, "Jewelry with a Texas Attitude," also boasts many unique pieces, composed of well-known symbols such as the Texas star, the longhorn and others. Stop by to see these and other award-winning designs firsthand at 325 S. Main St. For more information, visit www.thegreenbulljewelryco.com or call 830-249-7393. *(Color photo featured in front section of book.)*

AMERICAN INDIAN JEWELRY STORES
Member of the Indian Arts & Crafts Association

American Indian Jewelry Stores, established in 1988, purchases direct from Indian families. With two locations—one in Boerne at 126 S. Main St. and one in Bandera at 311 Main St.—they carry the largest selection of Native American jewelry and gifts in the Southwest at great prices. Both shops are filled with jewelry made by Hopi, Navajo and Zuni tribes using turquoise, onyx, malachite, spiney oyster and other stones set in sterling silver. They offer a large selection of rings, hair clips, concho belts, earrings and gift items, as well as bolo ties, money clips, knives and cuff links for men. American Indian Jewelry Stores are authorized Pendleton dealers. Spiritual souls will find a wonderful collection of medicine bags, healing stones and fragrant herbs. Art lovers will enjoy the limited edition prints, kachina dolls, handcrafted artifacts and tribal lore. Call 830-249-5766 or visit www.sunofabrave.com (Boerne), or call 830-796-4000 or visit www.americanindianjewelry.com (Bandera).

Restaurants & Special Events

GOLF RESORT & CONFERENCE CENTER

With panoramic views, spring-fed lakes and beautiful nature trails, Tapatio Springs Golf Resort & Conference Center is situated on a slice of heaven. Its beautiful locale is conveniently located at 314 Blue Heron Blvd. just minutes from Boerne, and that is only part of the story. Tapatio Springs' amenities—its outstanding golf courses, remarkable dining facilities and excellent special event facilities—are in a class by themselves. The original 18-hole golf course at Tapatio is known as "The Lakes and Valley Nines." In 1999, owner Jack Parker added the magnificent par-35 "Ridge Nine," which is as picturesque as it is challenging. Overlooking the ninth and 18th hole is the Blue Heron Restaurant, which features delicious steaks, seafood and continental fare, and its Sunday Brunch is a local favorite. Tapatio Springs is an excellent venue for corporate functions, special events and weddings. For reservations or information, call 800-973-8183 or visit www.tapatio.com. *(See related story on page 108.) (Color photo featured in front section of book.)*

They've put the "home cooking" back into restaurant food! The Hungry Horse Restaurant, 109 S. Saunders St. in Boerne, has been serving up delicious family-style meals in the Texas Hill Country since 1983. You'll be treated to a selection of many old favorites like scrumptious meat loaf, succulent chopped steak, delicious liver and onions, and award-winning chicken fried steak—so good that it was written up in *Texas Monthly* magazine.

You'll choose from three portion sizes, which accommodate all appetites, and a variety of dishes that will satisfy even the finickiest eaters. You can sample Hill Country traditions like fried green beans and fried broccoli, or stick with an American classic—the hamburger. Boerne locals can attest that the Hungry Horse serves the juiciest burgers in town. They're cooked-to-order with the tastiest onion rings this side of the border. Or if seafood or steaks stir your interest, the Hungry Horse offers fabulous seasoned grilled shrimp, fried or grilled catfish, rib eyes, T-bones and bacon-wrapped filets.

And for times when you don't feel like cooking, call to order a family meal-to-go that is sure to please everyone at home.

The Hungry Horse also provides catering services so you can bring the essence of home-style dining to your next gathering. The dedicated staff will customize your menu to reflect your personality and satisfy your budget.

The Hungry Horse has it all—affordable prices, a kid-friendly menu and weekday lunch and dinner specials offered by folks who care about you. Walking into the Hungry Horse is a refreshing journey back to a simpler time. For more information, call 830-816-8989 or visit www.hungryhorserestaurant.com.

Discover
New Braunfels / Gruene
/ Canyon Lake

New Braunfels is a remarkable mix of old and new—an authentic German community with a warm Texas drawl. Often referred to as the "City of a Prince," we know you will agree that it is also a "prince of a city." It is a place where you can soak in the natural beauty of the Texas Hill Country, explore historical sites, jump on a jet ski or get lost in a cave. You can dine at charming bier gartens, dance to oompah music, and fill up on flaky Strudel. New Braunfels has been called a city "where German heritage coexists with Texas lifestyle." This popular tourist town is now one of the state's top tourist destinations, featuring Schlitterbahn, the nation's largest and most popular water park; Natural Bridge Caverns, the state's largest caverns; a Wildlife Ranch and snake farm; wonderful shopping; and delicious authentic German food and culture. It is still a rather "old fashioned" town with a unique blend of two diverse cultures.

With the Comal and Guadalupe Rivers flowing through town, visitors can take advantage of fun-filled water activities such as fishing, swimming, boating or tubing. Coupled with great lodging choices, New Braunfels is the perfect place for memorable vacations. Within the New Braunfels area, you'll find the communities of **Gruene** and **Canyon Lake**, offering visitors everything from good ol' Texas country music to days of fun in the sun. Whether you are here with the girls for "A Lady's Day Out," or with the entire family for a fun Texas getaway, New Braunfels "wilkommens" all to stay and play, to shop and dine and to explore all of the wonderful treasures that make it a favorite Texas destination.

NEW BRAUNFELS

The "City of a Prince"

Prince Carl Fredrick Wilhelm Ludwig Georg Alfred Alexander of Solms-Braunfels, Germany, arrived in Texas in July 1844, searching for land for a group of German immigrants that would soon follow. When he found the tract of land near Comal Springs called "Las Fontanas" by the Mexicans, he knew that the beautiful, fertile region was perfect for the new settlers. He signed a deed to the land on March 15, 1845, and six days later, on March 21, 1845, his group of German farmers and craftsmen arrived and named the community New Braunfels in his honor. The first encampment was on the site of Sts. Peter and Paul Church, which is one of the oldest Catholic churches in Central Texas.

Even though the trip from Germany to New Braunfels proved harsh and life threatening for many pioneers, within five years of settling New Braunfels, it became an active center for commerce and was the fourth largest city in Texas. Many of the first German settlers were stone artisans, blacksmiths, brewers, millers, weavers, musicians, teachers and doctors, so it was no surprise that within a decade of its founding, New Braunfels, was an important agricultural market and manufacturing center.

In 1852 a German-Texan botanist named Ferdinand Lindheimer established and edited a German language newspaper called the New Braunfelser Zeitung, which he printed in his own home. Lindheimer became known as the Father of Texas Botany, with at least 32 native plants from Texas and Mexico bearing his name. History books tell us that during the Civil War a band of angry citizens stormed Lindheimer's house and threw his printing press into the Comal River. He immediately retrieved it and resumed printing. Lindheimer's home was donated to the New Braunfels Conservation Society and is open to the public.

You will also see evidence of New Braunfel's German heritage in some of the businesses that have operated continuously through the years within the same family, and in the street signs that bear the names of the first settlers.

New Braunfels Today

Because of New Braunfels' charming German heritage and culture, its close proximity to beautiful rivers and lakes, and its premier Hill Country locale, tourism became its major industry during the 20th century. Framed with historic buildings, the city's downtown district centers around Main Plaza, which has retained much of its early character and charm. A beautiful fountain, bronze sculptures and a music pavilion are center stage attractions in downtown and a place where locals and visitors gather for concerts and seasonal festivals, or just to relax and enjoy the beauty of the town. Some of the businesses in the downtown district have been there since the town was founded, such as Henne Hardware, Texas' oldest hardware store, and Naegelin's Bakery, also the oldest in the state. (Great German pastries!)

Of course, you can't visit downtown New Braunfels without enjoying the natural beauty of **Landa Park**, which is called "The Oasis of Texas." The park includes Comal Springs (the source of the Comal River), which gush from underground limestone formations throughout the park. In fact, it was because of this natural spring (originally called Las Fontanas) that Prince Carl decided to purchase the land here. The park was originally a private recreational area created by Henry Landa. The City of New Braunfels purchased the land in 1946, opening Landa Park to the public. On any day of the week you'll see families in paddle boats, rowboats and even glass bottom boats, or families picnicking under giant, ancient trees. There are nature trails, a miniature golf course, tennis courts and a challenging golf course. Plan to spend a beautiful day here in Landa Park.

History buffs will delight in the walking tour of New Braunfels' historical homes and businesses, but must plan time to see the **Sophienburg Museum**. The exhibits at the Sophienburg tell the unique story of this "City of a Prince," emphasizing the blending of the German, Native American, Hispanic and other cultures in New Braunfels. The Sophienburg Museum brings to life the early pioneers' struggles to survive and an early 1900's Main Street. The Archives is one of the largest collections of information that documents the German immigration to Texas, and is open to the public.

While visiting the Sophienburg Museum, you will learn how the name originated. When Prince Carl of Solms-Braunfels founded New Braunfels, he chose a hill overlooking the town as the site he intended for his "castle." His home would be called "Sophienburg" or "Sophia's Castle" for his fiancée, Lady Sophia, Princess of Salm-Salm. However, when she refused to make the trip to Texas, Prince Carl chose to return to Germany to be with her. (Texans still cannot understand this decision.) The Sophienburg is located on Prince Carl's Hill, 401 Coll St., (830-629-1900.)

You will feel as though you have stepped back in time, but you will also recognize that New Braunfels is a thriving community full of great opportunity for adventure and modern day excitement.

New Braunfels: An Adventure for the Little Ones

You'll enjoy the history of New Braunfels, delight in the great shopping and dining opportunities, and enjoy the blend of German and Texas cultures throughout the city. But, the kids want wet and wild adventure anywhere they go. So . . . head for any one of the city's well-known attractions that will provide hours of fun and excitement.

Schlitterbahn, called the nation's number one water park, attracts visitors from across the world to its surfing rides, uphill water coaster, tidal-wave river and tubing trails! Schlitterbahn began along the edge of a river in 1966, when Bob and Billye Henry and their children started building the water park, adding new attractions and accommodations each year. By the early 1990s, Schlitterbahn covered 6.5 acres, with hundreds of resort rooms, water slides and water playgrounds.

Natural Bridge Caverns, an incredible underground world of beauty, is one of the largest caverns in the state of Texas. Make reservations for the 75-minute tour through one-half mile of the spectacular cavern and see the amazing stalactites and stalagmites that are still growing! There are also more adventurous tours for the very brave.

Natural Bridge Wildlife Ranch is another great adventure especially for animal lovers. If you've ever dreamed of going on an African Safari, here's your chance. Wild animals from all over the

DISCOVER NEW BRAUNFELS / GRUENE / CANYON LAKE **125**

world roam freely within this beautiful, natural environment. You'll see giraffe, zebra, antelope and more in their home on the Texas Range.

Shop, Play, Dine, Stay in New **Braunfels**

Explore unique boutiques and vintage antique stores, shop the famous Henne Hardware, (even if you don't need hardware,) browse collectible shops and dazzling jewelry stores. Then, find a place to enjoy some of the most delicious German fare in the land. From small smokehouses and grills to sit-down, family-style restaurants and adorable tearooms, you'll find plenty of wonderful places to eat. Lodging choices are plentiful, and as unique as the city itself. Choose historic bed and breakfasts, plush hotels, luxury condominiums, or even a tennis ranch resort.

There are so many wonderful and exciting ways to spend your days in New Braunfels, especially if you are visiting during November. Wurstfest, rich in German culture and fun, is a ten-day festival and New Braunfels' best-known annual event. Enjoy potato pancakes, sausage on a stick, sweet strudel and fine Bavarian-style entertainment. You'll here these words often, "Come and habt spass!"

The locals invite visitors to, "Jump In, Dine In or Sleep In!" However you plan to do it, your stay in this charming Texas town with its German flair will be memorable and delicious!

GRUENE

One of the best ways to experience true Hill Country adventure is to spend a few days in Gruene. You can grab a tube and go with the flow of the cool Guadalupe River, dry off and have lunch on a deck overlooking the river, then get ready for a spin around the floor of Gruene Hall while enjoying great Texas country music.

Unlike many "ghost towns" that sprang up around New Braunfels that were unable to survive the grueling pioneer days, Gruene, dug its heels in and never gave up. Brothers Ernst Gruene, Jr., and Henry D. Gruene first established the Thornhill Stream Mills on the east bank of the Guadalupe River, and later Henry opened his own mercantile and general store. In 1882 he built a structure to serve as a dance pad, and today Gruene Hall is the oldest known dance hall in the entire state of Texas.

Although the town lost many of its residents and businesses during WWII and The Great Depression, Gruene Hall never closed. In 1974 a group of investors bought the community, and breathed new life into the town, mainly through the dance hall where country music legends attracted lots of visitors. The open-air dance floor, wood-burning stove and beautiful outdoor garden have remained virtually unchanged with time, and have been the center of Gruene's social activity through the years. In fact, the dance hall has hosted famous musicians like George Strait, Lyle Lovett, Merle Haggard, Garth Brooks, the Dixie Chicks and Willie Nelson. And, you might recognize it as the dance hall where John Travolta two-stepped around the dance floor as an angel in the movie, "Michael."

Shop 'n Dine

For such a small community, Gruene is big on entertainment, and that includes great shopping and dining opportunities. There are wonderful riverfront restaurants with incredible views, and charming downtown cafés, antique and specialty stores. Shopping is great any day in this tiny river town, but Gruene Market Days (every third weekend of the month except January) feature more than 100 artists' booths with crafts, antiques, gourmet foods and great entertainment.

CANYON LAKE & GUADALUPE RIVER

The people who live in and around Canyon Lake think that the area is one of the best-kept secrets of the Texas Hill Country. Sorry folks, it won't be for long! Canyon Lake (along with the Guadalupe River area) is called the "Water Recreation Capital of Texas," and its tranquil beauty beckons visitors from across the country as a premier vacation spot or second home. Canyon Lake and the Guadalupe River together make up the heart of the Texas Hill Country, and offer recreational fun through every season. There are boat and watercraft rentals, hiking trails, river- rafting rides, bird watching, fine shopping and dining opportunities and even "dinosaur tracks to explore!" You can sail into the sunset, charter a romantic cocktail cruise, grab a tube for floating fun or try your luck at something more adventurous like kayaking or scuba diving.

Canyon Lake and the nearby communities (Sattler, Hancock, Cranes Mill and Startzville) are known for breathtaking waterfront and Hill Country views. The lake covers more than 8,200 acres and is one of the most beautiful and scenic lakes in Texas. Located just 40 miles north of San Antonio and 25 minutes from New Braunfels, Canyon Lake is convenient to both large-city opportunities and peaceful Hill Country serenity.

The First Inhabitants?!!!!

Paleontologists tell us that during the Crustacean Period (part of the Mesozoic Era—more than 100 million years ago!) most of Central Texas was covered by a shallow sea from the Gulf of Mexico to the Arctic Ocean. Our beautiful "Hill Country" was then a low-lying area of marsh and algae-covered mud. Scientists believe that dinosaurs left footprints in the mud, which were then filled in with sediment. Over time, these filled indentions turned to stone and were buried for millions of years. Acrocanthosaurus or Iguanidon dinosaur prints were found during the early 1980s in the Canyon Lake area, when land was being cleared for an RV park. The John Parker Family dedicated the site of the dinosaur footprints to the **Heritage Museum of the Texas Hill Country**, which opened in 2002. The Museum also has exhibits featuring the Native Americans of the area and early 19th century pioneers (Indian artifacts, old farm machinery, fossil displays and Canyon Lake Dam history archives).

A "Gorgeous" Gorge

Be sure to visit the Canyon Lake Gorge as well for additional insight into the geology of the Texas Hill Country limestone formations in Comal County. This "gorgeous" gorge was literally carved or cut into the landscape when floodwaters escaped over the Spillway during the Flood of 2002. This was the first time that the floodwaters flowed over the Emergency Spillway since the dam was completed in 1964. The runoff water that poured into the Canyon

Reservoir was at least three and one-half times the amount of water that the Reservoir is able to hold. The 2002 flood wreaked havoc on the Canyon Lake area, but in the end it proved to be a huge gift from Mother Nature. When everything settled, the water had cut into the earth through layers of sediment and time, revealing dinosaur prints, fossils and natural springs and pools. The finds were priceless. The Gorge Preservation Society (GPS) was formed to develop and manage the gorge, with plans to expand it into one of the areas' most popular tourist attractions. The gorge is a testament to the power of water to change our earth. It will provide scientists with a wealth of geologic information about this area's prehistoric age. For information on gorge tours, visit www.canyongorge.org.

For additional information about New Braunfels and Gruene, contact the Greater New Braunfels Chamber of Commerce and Visitors Center at 830-625-2385, 800-572-2626 or visit www.nbcham.org.

For additional information on Canyon Lake and the Guadalupe River, contact the Canyon Lake Area Chamber of Commerce at 830-964-2223, 800-528-2104 or visit www.canyonlakechamber.com.

New Braunfels Gruene / Canyon Lake Fairs Festivals & Fun

February
Old Gruene Market Days
Gospel Brunch
Country Doll Show & Sale
Canyon Lake Winter Texas
  Reception
Canyon Lake Senior Prom

March
Old Gruene Market Days
Gospel Brunch
Spring Sidewalk Sale
Rio Guadalupe Music Fest
ACCOG Spring Lake / River
  Cruise

April
Old Gruene Market Days
Gospel Brunch
Folkfest
Kindermasken Parade
Wein & Saengerfest
Canyon Lake Market Days
Canyon Lake Area BBQ

May
Old Gruene Market Days
Gospel Brunch
American Music Jam

June
Old Gruene Market Days
Gospel Brunch

July
Old Gruene Market Days
Gospel Brunch
Independence Day Parade
Canyon Lake Serve & Protect
Fireworks over Canyon Lake
Classic Car Cruise-in

August
Old Gruene Market Days
Gospel Brunch

September
Old Gruene Market Days
Gospel Brunch
Comal County Fair Parade
Sunfish Labor Day Regatta
Classic Car Cruise-in
Texas Metal Arts Festival
Canyon Lake Freedom Walk

October
Old Gruene Market Days
Gospel Brunch
Gruene Music & Wine Fest
Canyon Lake Heritage Museum
  Harvestfest
Clay Festival
Canyon Lake market Days

November
Old Gruene Market Days
Gospel Brunch
Wurstfest
Fall Sidewalk Sale
Downtown Tree Lighting
Weinachtsmarkt
Classic Car Cruise-in

December
Old Gruene Market Days
Gospel Brunch
Christmas Along the Corridor
Gruene Town Lighting
Pony Express Ride
Wassailfest

FAITHVILLE

If Darlene McIntosh can offer just two words of advice to anyone it would be, "Have Faith!" Her unfaltering faith in God's promises for her life led her to open the Gathering Place Tea Room in Spring Branch. It has become the center of a collection of unique shops called Faithville. Enjoy a relaxing stroll under the oaks, have a delicious lunch, and then browse the charming collection of boutiques. There is even a restored chapel where you can listen to inspirational music or pray.

Gathering Place Tea Room serves "heavenly" fare, from delicious appetizers to fresh salads, soups and sandwiches, and wonderful homemade breads and desserts. Call 830-885-6388 or visit www.gatheringplaceatfaithville.com. (See related story on page 169.)

Cristal's, with two other locations including this one in Faithville, is a fun and stylish collection of ladies apparel and accessories, including lines like Tummy Tuck Jeans and ZoZo. Call 830-885-2394. (See related story on page 156.)

Sassy Spur, like its name, is a hip boutique that features unusual gifts, kitchenware, fashion accessories and Shabby Chic treasures, as well as refurbished cowhide antiques. Call 830-885-4832. (See related story on page 157.)

Two Chic Chicks, originally an online store, is an all-inclusive bridal, special occasion and gift boutique, with handmade fine jewelry and a signature candle collection. Call 830-885-2699 or visit www.two-chic-chicks.com. (See related story on page 155.)

Lady Jane's, a delightful gift boutique with wonderful home décor, jewelry, fashion accessories and lots of great children's items. This is a fun store with an ever-changing inventory. Call 830-885-5437. (See related story on page 164.)

These unique businesses and more are located at Faithville in Spring Branch at 17130 Hwy. 46 W. Stop, shop, eat, relax and enjoy!

Antiques

DOWNTOWN ANTIQUE MALL

If you're a die-hard antiquer, there is a wonderful shopping experience in downtown New Braunfels that you won't want to miss. Downtown Antique Mall, located at 209 W. San Antonio St., is 12,000 square feet of antiques and collectibles. Fifty dealers offer everything from jewelry, toys, books, glassware, china, linens, silver, chandeliers, breweriana and furniture to vintage memorabilia from the 30s, 40s, 50s and 60s. Downtown Antique Mall is located in a beautiful turn-of-the-20th century building that has its original wood floor and tin ceiling. It was remodeled in 2005 to give you an even better shopping experience. It's within walking distance of many interesting shops, allowing you to make a day of it. So grab your girlfriends or loved ones and head to the Downtown Antique Mall. Visit www.downtownantiquemall.com or call 830-620-7223 for more information.

AUSTIN'S GENERAL STORE

After the success of Christy Sebby's specialty store, Christy's Jewelry & Treasures, the time was right to expand and open a second store in Canyon Lake. Named after her son, Austin's General Store, 15551 FM 306, is the kind of place you can browse for hours. Christy grew up in the retail business watching her mother manage and own fine gift and jewelry stores. Christy inherited an eye for detail and display, but she gives most of the credit for the store's charm to her husband Todd. Tucked amid the wonderful antiques and rich décor you'll find unusual treasures. There is also a great display of gourmet foods, intriguing cookbooks and kitchen tools. This store has old-time appeal, quality merchandise and great prices, and the friendly owners make it an all-around fun place to shop! Call 830-964-4606. *(See related story on page 157.)*

Artists & Art Galleries

Sattler Artisans' Alley
Art, Hand crafts, Home Decor & More

Canyon Lake has proven to be the perfect place for the wonderful collection of artisans and crafters that make up Sattler Artisans' Alley, 1381 Sattler Rd., Pamela and Barry Dorfman opened the art gallery and café as a venue for artists and crafters to display and sell their artwork in the Texas Hill Country. Pamela's experience as a high school educator and director of high school, university and community theatre productions, as well as Barry's extensive experience in sales and marketing, combine perfectly to create and manage this remarkable art gallery. In fact, it was Barry's love of quality wood furniture that peaked interest in opening the gallery in the first place.

Mimicking the "Market Days" of nearby towns like Wimberley, Fredericksburg and Gruene, the artists offer one-of-a-kind hand-crafted items from jewelry to custom-tooled leather, as well as home décor accessories. And, don't miss Barry's handcrafted, quality pine furniture and accessories. Art classes in every media are also available, as well as, classes in folk art such as gourd crafting, mosaics, quilting, jewelry and more. Visitors will also find a delicious assortment of Kewpie's jams and jellies that are unique to Central Texas plus the delightful fragrances of Soy Sisters' Candles.

More than an art gallery and showcase for handcrafted creations, Sattler Artisans' Alley is an inviting place to share a soothing cup of coffee or tea, a refreshing fruit smoothie, or a tasty Italian gelato with friends at the Lewis B.'s Artisan Gelato & Sorbetto Café. Or, bring your laptop and chat on the Internet.

Four artists came on board at Artisans' Alley in the beginning—today there are more than 38 artisans represented, and their stunning, creative work is waiting to inspire you. For more information, call 830-964-3609 or visit www.sartisansalley.com. *(Color photo featured in front section of book.)*

Attractions, Entertainment & Museums

BRAUNTEX PERFORMING ARTS THEATRE

The cultural experience that is breathing life into downtown New Braunfels has its audiences literally dancing in the aisles. The Brauntex Performing Arts Theatre, built in 1941, operated as the Brauntex Movie Theatre until 1998. After the building's renovations to accommodate live theatrical productions, it reopened its doors in 2000, offering entertainment from touring artists and many local performing arts groups. The Brauntex Performing Arts Theatre Association now presents as many as 10 professional touring productions annually, and local theatre groups use the theatre as well. The Brauntex can also be rented to businesses and civic organizations for conferences, and reception space is available for weddings, reunions and special events. Look for the historic neon sign at 290 W. San Antonio St. Call 830-627-0808 or visit www.brauntex.org.

An African Safari—Texas Style! Damaraland zebra, watusi, gemsbok, kudu, springbok, wapiti and barasingha. These beautiful animals look as exotic as their names, and although they hail from as far away as India and Africa, you can see them all right here at the Natural Bridge Wildlife Ranch in between New Braunfels and San Antonio. The family-operated Wildlife Ranch is located on a registered Texas Land Heritage Property at 26515 Natural Bridge Cavern Rd., which has been in the same family for more than 100 years (six generations!). The Wildlife Center opened to the public in 1984, and it is now the most visited and longest running safari drive-thru park in Texas.

As you drive through the picturesque Hill Country pastures, you will get the chance to see and feed many of the exotic animals on the property. Hundreds of exotic, endangered and native species roam freely on the ranch, so be sure to bring your camera. There are 19-foot giraffes, striped zebras, graceful gazelles, two-hump camels, Cape buffalo, curious ostriches, African lemurs, American bison and much more. The animals will come right up to the vehicle to eat, and some will even try to poke their heads inside if they don't get their fair share.

Little ones will love the Walk-A-Bout tour, which includes a petting zoo, picnic area, gift shop and gazebo shaped structure home to exotic birds and primates. Feeding here is encouraged, and babies are delivered throughout the year, which gives visitors a personal experience with the miracle of nature.

A trip to the Natural Bridge Wildlife Ranch will prove to be an exciting adventure for the entire family (even if you will be the one in the cage!). For information on hours or reservations, call 830-438-7400 or visit www.WildlifeRanchTexas.com.

Listed as one of "Ten Great Places" by *USA Today*, Natural Bridge Caverns definitely lives up to its reputation for excitement and adventure. Located between New Braunfels and San Antonio at 26495 Natural Bridge Caverns Rd., it is the largest cavern in Texas and attracts more than 250,000 visitors each year. The Cavern was discovered in 1960 by a group of college students from St. Mary's University in San Antonio. After crawling through two miles of vast cavern passage under the 60-foot limestone bridge, they discovered what is today the North Cavern—one of the world's premier show caverns. A 75-minute tour of this cavern takes visitors through enormous underground rooms with delicate crystalline formations and gigantic stone monuments. Visit the Jaremy Room or take a flashlight tour through the South Cavern and see The Soda Straw crystal formations. Don't miss the "Wild Cave Tour" this adventure requires caving and rappelling gear and lots of adventurous spirit. For the ultimate adventure, climb the Watchtower, hook onto the zip line, and soar at speeds up to 25 m.p.h. So much adventure and excitement! For information call, 210-651-6101 or visit www.naturalbridgecaverns.com

TEXANA–LAND FUN PARK AT LAKEVIEW RESORT

Debbie and Loren Drum have completed a full renovation of their remarkable Drums' Lakeview Resort in Canyon Lake with a fabulous addition of their very own water park. Texana-Land Fun Park is located at 872 Ledgerock Dr. across from the Resort. The park features The Stampede Bumper Boat Pool, waterfalls and grotto. Float or tube The Happy Trails Lazy River or try your skills at miniature golf. Debbie says, "I envisioned it as a place where parents can come and relax while their children play in the water park." With the meeting area and game room, Texana-Land is the perfect place for great birthday parties and celebrations. Call 830-899-7007, 800-385-4013 or visit www.drumresorts.com. *(See related story on page 147.) (Color photo featured in front section of book.)*

NEW BRAUNFELS CONSERVATION SOCIETY

Conservation Plaza • Lindheimer House

In 1845, Prince Carl of Solms-Braunfels gifted 2 ½ acres of land on the Comal River to Ferdinand Lindheimer in appreciation for his efforts in leading settlers to the area. Lindheimer, who is known as the "Father of Texas Botany," built a house on the land in 1852. When one of Lindheimer's granddaughters (Mrs. Sida Simon Martin) offered the historic home, 491 Comal Ave., as a gift to the city in 1964, the New Braunfels Conservation Society was born. The organization has been successfully preserving and maintaining many of the city's historical buildings ever since.

The Society is most proud of the accumulation of 14 Fachwerk buildings (circa 1849-1870) that have been relocated, restored and furnished to form a German Village called Conservation Plaza. Unlike the Lindheimer home, which sits in its original location, these 14 buildings stood in the way of progress and had to be moved. The Society acquired the Carl Friedrich Baetge house, the Welsch Barn, the Star Exchange Saloon, the Blank limestone house, the Haelbig Music Studio, the one-room limestone Church Hill School Building, and the cabinet maker Jahn's house and cabinet shop. If not for the efforts of the Society in moving these historic buildings to Conservation Plaza, many would have been torn down in the name of progress and a piece of Texas history would have been lost forever. The Forke Store and Rose Conservatory and Gazebo are also in the village at 1300 Church Hill Dr,—with more than 50 varieties of Antique Roses. Springtime is delightful with the beautiful blooms and heavenly aroma.

Tours are available, and many of these special sites host weddings, receptions and other special events. Visit www.nbconservation.org or call 830-629-2943 for more information.

(See related story on page 142.)

Bakeries

NAEGELIN'S BAKERY
Texas' Oldest and Finest
—— SINCE 1868 ——
ON THE SQUARE

In 1868, Edouard Naegelin, a young man of only 24 years, arrived in New Braunfels with a sack of flour and less than one dollar. This Alsace-Lorraine native had already co-owned a bakery in San Antonio, but he desired to have one of his own. He opened his first New Braunfels' bakery on the site that is now City Hall. In 1870, he moved to the present location at 129 S. Seguin St. and you'll be thrilled to know that it's still operating today.

Generations have enjoyed the warm aroma and delectable freshness that Naegelin's Bakery has to offer. As Texas' oldest and continually running bakery, it is a New Braunfels' staple. The current owners, the Granzin family, renovated the bakery in the 1980s but they continue to use the same tried-and-true recipes that Naegelin and his family created. Patrons are treated to straight-from-the-oven baked goods like Lebkuchen (a popular German, frosted cookie), breads, cakes, pies and the bakery's specialty—apple strudel. Nolan Ryan receives an apple strudel every Christmas. Other scrumptious German, French and Danish pastries are baked daily too. The endless choices are sure to satisfy even the pickiest sweet tooth.

The Granzin family continues to build on the quality goods and superb customer service that Naegelin's loyal regulars have come to expect. Naegelin's bakes a wide selection of cakes—all different varieties for all different occasions. People across the country have enjoyed Naegelin's baked goods, especially its Bear Claws. Thankfully, Naegelin's ships anywhere in the continental US, so visitors can have the homemade goodness shipped to them. For more information, call 830-625-5722, 877-788-2895 or visit www.naegelins.com. *(See related stories on pages 145 and 167.)*

Bed & Breakfasts, Cottages, Hotels, Inns, Rentals & Resorts

KUEBLER WALDRIP HAUS & DANVILLE SCHOOLHOUSE BED & BREAKFAST

In 1974, when the Waldrip family purchased the property that became the Kuebler Waldrip Haus B & B, they were only the third family to occupy the house since Andreas and Katherine Pape built it in 1847. Today, it is one of the most outstanding bed and breakfasts in Texas. Larry and Margaret and their three sons—Dibrell, Darrell and David—created a place that guests describe as "magical and restful." Perfectly located on 43 relaxing Hill Country acres just minutes from the Guadalupe and Comal rivers, Schlitterbahn, entertainment in historic New Braunfels and Gruene, Margaret and her son, Darrell operate the Kuebler Waldrip Haus, which is absolutely perfect for getaways, vacations, church and corporate retreats, family reunions, and weddings.

Relax and enjoy the wildlife and pet cats, the sweet country air, the history of the buildings, and the hospitality of this delightful family. Guests vow that the breakfasts are "the best in Texas" and are worth the trip themselves. Scrumptious egg dishes, delectable sausage, fresh fruit, fluffy biscuits, and decadent cinnamon rolls are regulars at their table.

Accommodations sleep 22-34 in three luxuriously restored and enlarged buildings. The Kuebler Waldrip Haus, an 1847 hand-hewn limestone homestead has fireplaces, five lovely bedrooms and five baths. Recycled rocks from a local church and the Comal County Jail made beautiful additions. The 1863 Danville Schoolhouse features the original chalkboard and wood floors. With four bedrooms, five baths, large meeting room, kitchen, piano and 48" TV with VCR/DVD, this building is perfect for group events. And, Deer Haven Cottage is a cozy three-bedroom cottage named for Angel (the pet deer) that insisted on standing right in the middle of the old barn's restoration.

The Kuebler Waldrip Haus and Danville Schoolhouse Bed and Breakfast, located at 1620 Hueco Springs Loop, is one-of-a-kind. For more information, call 830-625-8300, 800-299-8372 or visit www.kueblerwaldrip.com. Hablamos español.

FIREFLY INN BED & BREAKFAST

Sometimes everyone needs to get away from the hustle and bustle of life. And when you do, it's nice to know that someone else will handle all the details. Firefly Inn Bed & Breakfast is just the place. This gorgeous Texas Hill Country retreat, located at 120 Naked Indian Tr. in Canyon Lake, will wrap around you like a warm hug. Situated on four acres, its private cottages feature all sorts of things to pamper you—iron beds, Jacuzzi tubs and fully equipped kitchens. Owners Jack and Kathy Tipton will make your time at Firefly as relaxing as possible. Each morning, Kathy delivers a full breakfast right to your door, and she even accommodates special dietary needs. Located just minutes from New Braunfels, Gruene and the Guadalupe River, you can choose your entertainment. You may even see some Texas wildlife! For more information, call 830-905-3989, 800-687-2887 or visit www.fireflyinn.com.

GreensKeeper Inn

GreensKeeper Inn is a stately Victorian-Style Inn at 451 Watts Ln., overlooking the 9th Fairway on Canyon Lake Golf Club in the beautiful Texas Hill Country, where you can enjoy feeding the whitetail deer right from the back deck! The rooms are furnished with lovely antiques and luxurious bedding, aromatherapy candles and cable TV/DVD, and each has a private bathroom. Guests love the idea that breakfast is served at their leisure just a short walk down the cart path at the Clubhouse. You can reserve individual rooms or the entire Inn, which sleeps as many as 20—perfect for family reunions!

The Innkeeper, Karen Watson planned (and dreamed) that one day, as the last child left for college, she would be feathering her "empty nest" by transforming her beautiful home into a bed and breakfast. Karen absolutely loves her new role in life! She loves meeting new people, making new friends, decorating and staying busy—the ideal recipe for a successful Innkeeper!

As a guest at the Inn, you are in the midst of numerous and varied choices of entertainment, fine dining and activities that are sure to please all! You can enjoy the pool or golfing at the Club, and in the evening kick up your heels at Gruene Hall—the oldest Dance Hall in Texas! Or, as her motto states, "Relax, take time to enjoy life!" GreensKeeper Inn is only a short drive to the Comal or Guadalupe rivers for boating, fishing or tubing. One of the nicest things

about staying at GreensKeeper Inn is knowing that Karen donates a portion of your reservation to an organization call Orphan Helpers (www.orphanhelpers.org). For more information, visit www.GreensKeeperInn.com or call 210-825-7461, 877-473-0950.

Lamb's Rest Inn
Bed and Breakfast

There is something so healing about being surrounded by beautiful landscapes, and at Lamb's Rest Inn, 1385 Edwards Blvd. in New Braunfels, healing and serenity is what it's all about. This tranquil getaway is situated right on the Guadalupe River. Owners George and Judy Rothell have created a sanctuary like no other. Judy, an accomplished gardener, has worked tirelessly to establish a lush garden of fragrant herbs and intoxicating flowers. At Lamb's Rest Inn you can choose from six unique rooms. During your stay, you are treated to only the best—luxurious linens, Jacuzzi tubs, in-room fireplaces and gourmet breakfasts. You can relax in a hammock, fish from the deck, explore nearby Historic Gruene or take a dip in the river—whatever rejuvenates you. For more information, call 830-609-3932, 888-609-3932 or visit www.lambsrestinn.com.

Gerlich-Wagenfuehr Bed and Breakfast

One of the treasures of the New Braunfels Conservation Society is the charming Gerlich-Wagenfuehr Bed and Breakfast, located in downtown New Braunfels at 505 W. San Antonio St. It was built in 1858, and boasts a large living room, dining room, sitting room, bedroom and bath. It can sleep four with the living room sleeper sofa. A microwave, coffee pot, refrigerator and TV/VCR are provided for your comfort and convenience. This historic home is located just minutes from Conservation Plaza, shopping and dining opportunities. For more information, call 830-626-7295, 830-629-2943 or visit www.nbconservation.org.
(See related story on page 137.)

BARNSIDE LODGING

Built in the style of early Texas barns, and nestled under giant live oak and wild cherry trees, Barnside Lodging is one of the Texas Hill Country's most enchanting rustic retreats. Owners Ron and Lil Mitchell designed each cabin with reclaimed barn wood, bead board, tin and architectural treasures salvaged from the historic Bergheim and Huber homesteads. The buildings once housed Ron's handmade furniture and woodwork but have been converted into warm spaces that will rejuvenate even the weariest traveler. The rooms are decorated with Ron's one-of-a-kind handmade barn furniture and Lil's award-winning watercolors. Each is furnished with kitchen supplies, a TV, Wi-Fi and linens. Barnside Lodging, 19827 FM 306, is a quiet retreat that allows visitors to enjoy activities on nearby Canyon Lake. And, boat parking is available at each cabin. For more information, call 830-935-2110 or visit www.barnsidelodging.com.

Prince Solms Inn
Bed & Breakfast

This incredible historic bed and breakfast has become one of Texas' most famous and prized landmarks. The Prince Solms Inn Bed & Breakfast, 295 E. San Antonio St. was built in 1898 by Emilie Eggeling, an early settler of New Braunfels. The majestic two-story Inn was crafted with handmade bricks and cypress milled on the banks of the Guadalupe River. The main Inn features two luxury suites and eight beautifully furnished guest rooms, all with private baths. Also located on the property is the New Braunfels Feed Store, which was built in 1860, and restored in 2000 to offer three large guest rooms. The Joseph Klein House, built in 1852 sits just behind the Inn and is a perfect cottage getaway while enjoying this beautiful and charming town. A scrumptious full country breakfast is served each morning in the dining room, on the patio, or in the comfort of your suite. Call 830-625-9169, 800-625-9169 or visit www.princesolmsinn.com.

MISS RUBY'S
Guest Haus

Whether you are in town to float the river, poke around in the area's great antique and gift shops or just enjoy the beauty and charm of the Texas Hill Country, we've found the perfect place to settle in for the evening. Miss Ruby's Guest Haus is located just off the Guadalupe River in Historic Gruene. This wonderful home sleeps nine people, and is just upstream from Gruene Dance Hall where music drifts in on the breeze. A tin-covered front porch looks out onto a beautiful entertainment area with outdoor cooking facilities and seating that is the perfect place to dine under the Texas stars. The Guest Haus is decorated in the comfortable Texas Coastal style, and has amenities like cable TV in each room and a fridge stocked with dips, snacks and beverages. If you need a larger place for the crew, ask about Miss Ruby's Castle that sleeps 16. Be sure to wander down to Miss Ruby's Gift Shop for a truly unique shopping experience. In fact, there is a party on the patio every weekend! For more information, call 830-832-8555 or visit www.missrubys.com. *(See related story on page 163.)*

──── GRUENE RIVER INN ────

Breath-taking, panoramic views stretch out from the private balconies of the Gruene River Inn. This gorgeous retreat, located at 1111 Gruene Rd., is perched 100 feet above the Guadalupe River. Each of its 14 rooms is named after Texas rivers, and they reflect all the charm and comfort that the Texas Hill Country has to offer (including private Jacuzzi baths!). Owners Bill Evans and Walter and Danita Hayes owned another area business, but in 2004 the opportunity arose for them to buy the Gruene River Inn. It was a chance they couldn't pass up. They will pamper you with true Texas hospitality. Each morning they serve an extended continental breakfast, and there is room for larger gatherings on the covered deck. The Inn is located within walking distance of downtown Historic Gruene where you'll enjoy shopping, restaurants and live music. Call 830-627-1600 or visit www.grueneriverinn.com.

NAEGELINS HAUS BED & BREAKFAST

Right off the downtown square at 131 S. Seguin St. is the oldest home in its original location in New Braunfels—and it houses Naegelins Haus, a cozy bed and breakfast. Naegelins Haus was built in 1845 and is a Texas heritage landmark, which still has the original pine floors and faux work on the front exterior and interior walls. While it has a long history, Naegelins Haus is updated with all the finest fixtures. Guests are also treated to soft goose down blankets, lush 600-thread-count sheets, fluffy pillows, and luxurious Turkish towels. Breakfast is enjoyed next door at Naegelin's Bakery, Texas' oldest bakery. Visit www.naegelinshaus.com or call 830-822-6174. *(See related stories on pages 138 and 167.)*

Gruene Mansion Inn

Cecil Eager, former coach and Athletic Director at Abilene Christian University, used to visit Gruene as often as possible with his wife Judi. They were fascinated by the Gruene Mansion Inn and eventually purchased this historic landmark. It has been a wonderful adventure—and a divine decision—for this hospitable couple. The Gruene Mansion Inn was built by Henry D. Gruene in 1872 and is a lovely German-Victorian-Texas style inn located at 1275 Gruene Rd. on the banks of the Guadalupe River. *Texas Highways* magazine readers voted it one of the Top 10 Most Popular Country Inns/B&B's and *Arrington Publications* readers named it one of the Most Romantic Inns. You can choose from 31 rooms located in six buildings. The delicious breakfast, served each morning by the delightful staff, consists of homemade pastries, fresh fruit and their celebrated Jalapeno Pie and Country Casserole. Enjoy your breakfast in your room, in the dining room, or on the patio. For more information, visit www.gruenemansioninn.com or call 830-629-2641.

HIDEOUT
ON THE HORSESHOE

Imagine waking up to sunlight streaming through the windows of your own private cabin. You tiptoe out of bed, walk to the window and take in the gorgeous view. Breathing deeply, you feel the stress of life slowly wash away. At Hideout on the Horseshoe, breath-taking views, natural landscapes and plush accommodations pamper you from head to toe. It's truly an experience for those who want to take in the beauty of the outdoors without sacrificing luxury.

Each of the Hideout's 18 spectacular cabins overlooks the famous Horseshoe Loop on the Guadalupe River. Glorious views of the river surround you. In fact, the entire riverside of each cabin has a continuously running covered porch! And the cabins are as first-class as the views. Featuring one, two and three-bedroom cabins with queen-size beds, full-size refrigerators, copper sinks, fireplaces, flat-screen satellite TVs and Wi-Fi. When has roughing it ever been this fun?

If you want to get up close and personal with the river, the Horseshoe can help you with that too. You can access it directly from the resort, or if you want to float down the river, the Hideout offers tube rental and shuttle service.

This beautiful resort is private enough for a romantic getaway for two, but it's also great for families and group events. Whether you're looking to plan a wedding, conference or graduation party, the Hideout is a perfect choice. It has horseshoe pits, gas and coal grills, an outdoor fireplace and even a children's play area. When you're ready to dine and shop, you're only 10 minutes from downtown Historic Gruene.

Hideout on the Horseshoe, at 515 FM 2673, books quickly so don't wait. Grab your girlfriends or your family and plan your next getaway now. Visit www.floattheguadalupe.com or call 830-964-4540, 888-405-4433 for more information. *(Color photo featured in front section of book.)*

Drums' LAKEVIEW RESORT

Breathtaking Hill Country views, secluded surroundings, friendly whitetail deer, winding nature trails, cozy cabins and even a whimsical "treehouse!" Drums' Lakeview Resort, 872 Ledgerock Dr., is as wonderful as it sounds, and a favorite place for family vacations or romantic getaways.

Debbie and Loren Drum own and manage this remarkable resort, which is located where the old "fishing lodge" was built when Canyon Lake was developed in 1960. The peaceful hideaway features condos that overlook the lake, with full kitchens and private baths. If you want a little more privacy, there are also six cabins with cedar siding, copper roofing, hand-cut deck railings, fireplaces and hot tubs nestled along the nature trails that run through the ravines and into the cove. Kids, young and old, can enjoy floating the lazy river or riding in the bumper boats at Texana-Land Fun Park, built right on the property.

For a fantasy adventure that rivals your dreams of living like the Robinson family in a treehouse, the Drums have created an escape that is actually a fortress in the treetops. The Treehouse Lodge is an incredible structure that is built around enormous pecan and cypress trees and features a tower that soars eight stories high! Guests have access to decks with views of the river below and the wildlife. The lodge can be divided suitably for guest groups, or used as a bed & breakfast for couples. This is truly one of the most amazing places you will ever stay!

The Drums are such interesting people with backgrounds and interests that make them perfect resort hosts. Loren is a former Olympic pentathlete and an engineer—who designed the Treehouse Lodge. Debbie is a gourmet cook, and the guests enjoy her homemade treats each day. And both are avid historians and collectors of Native American artifacts. Call 830-899-7007, 800-385-4013 or visit www.drumresorts.com, to live out those childhood fantasies! *(See related story on page 136.) (Color photo featured in front section of book.)*

THE HOTEL FAUST

In October of 1929 The Faust Hotel opened its doors for the first time in the small German town of New Braunfels, which is comfortably situated between the larger cities of San Antonio and Austin. Originally known as the Travelers Hotel it was soon renamed The Faust in honor of Walter Faust, Sr. No expense was spared in the creation of this charming boutique hotel with its Spanish Renaissance tiled floors and unique handcrafted furniture. The Faust Hotel boasts of 62 rooms including two suites. Each room is furnished with antiques but containing all of today's modern amenities. It is the perfect location for any event whether that is a wedding in the Grand Ballroom or just a romantic evening in the Honeymoon suite. Located conveniently downtown at 240 S. Seguin Ave., the Historic Faust Hotel awaits your arrival! For more information, call 830-625-7791 or visit www.fausthotel.com.

When planning your next family vacation or getaway, consider one of the most impressive resorts in Texas—T Bar M Resort. This premier destination offers guests the services of a three-star resort without the big price. Accommodations include secluded Sunday House cottages and condominiums, a 74-room country inn, convenient tennis villas and rustic log cabins. Visitors can enjoy a variety of indoor and outdoor activities like swimming, tennis, horseshoes, basketball, ping-pong, volleyball, pool and air-hockey. There is also a first-rate fitness center, and guests can schedule spa treatments in their rooms. The entire family will enjoy T Bar M, because there is something for everyone. Great food, a friendly staff, fabulous outdoor fun—all on 160 acres of beautiful Texas Hill Country in New Braunfels at 2549 Hwy. 46 W. For more information, call 830-625-7738, 800-292-5469 or visit www.tbarm.com. *(See related story on page 177.)*

Scenic River Properties

Bridget McDougall grew up swimming, fishing and playing in the beautiful Guadalupe River. After living in Houston and abroad for many years, she and her husband Shelby hightailed it back to the Texas Hill Country as fast as they could, and founded Scenic River Properties in 1990. Bridget says, "We opened three pink and white houses on River Road, and they were booked for the summer before we even finished construction!" Today, Scenic River Properties manages more than 23 houses along the Guadalupe River and Canyon Lake—perfect for fabulous, memorable Hill Country vacations. Whether you need a hideaway for a weekend shopping trip, a corporate event locale or a summer-of-fun getaway for your whole family, Bridget offers quality, fully furnished houses for both short and long-term rentals. Scenic River Properties is located at 1295 Sattler Rd. in Sattler. For more information, call 830-964-3127, 800-765-7077 or visit www.scenicriverproperties.com.

(See related story on page 166.)

Camping, RVing & Cabins

If you have never "floated the river," you should add this Adventure to the top of your to-do list. Clear and crisp, even in summer, the lower Guadalupe River is fed from the bottom of Canyon Lake, which averages a chilly 57 degrees. So, tubing and rafting are two of the best ways to stay cool and enjoy the beautiful Texas Hill Country. Mountain Breeze Camp at 201 Mountain Breeze Camp Rd. in Canyon Lake is a wonderful destination for this Texas size treat. The campground offers overnight accommodations but also is a full-service river outfitter, furnishing rafts, tubes and inflatable canoes. The main building was originally used as a fishing lodge in the 1950s and today serves as a bar area with pool tables and a small store. However, anglers still find an abundance of trout, bass and perch in the river. Riverfront campsites, rustic log cabins, bathhouses, swimming pool and barbecue grills are available for guests. Owner Paul Rich is proud to offer families and groups a wonderful spot to unwind, float the river, enjoy delicious burgers and beer, play a game of darts, or just enjoy the view of the rugged hills "rising from the river." For more information, call 830-964-2484 or visit www.mountainbreezecamp.com.

Pack your bathing suit, put up your tent or park your RV, grab a tube and get ready for one of the most memorable vacations you will ever experience at the Lazy L & L Campground on River Road. Located near Canyon Lake on acres of beautiful Guadalupe River frontage, 11 miles outside of New Braunfels, this family-owned-and-operated campground has been hosting families for more than 35 years. Louis and Viola Meckel opened the gates of the Lazy L & L, welcoming tubers in 1972, and today their daughter and son-in-law, Margie and Rodney Skolaut, continue the legacy of wonderful family fun on the river and enjoyment of the beautiful surroundings.

Lazy L & L includes three areas: primitive tent camping, a Group area, and the Main Campground. They offer full RV hookups, riverfront tent camping, tubing and rafting river trips. It is also home to "Devil's Playground," one of the best areas for whitewater rapids on the entire Guadalupe River. All of the RV sites have 30/50-amp electrical service and the lots are large enough to easily accommodate Big Rigs with slide-outs. Each site has a picnic table, barbecue grill and a fire ring for a campfire, and hot showers are available to all campers. The Grill is open on weekends during the summer months, or you can pickup drinks, snacks, ice, coolers and toiletries at the Camp Store. They can even cater a special event

Generations of families have returned year after year to the Lazy L & L for family vacations, but it has also become a popular spot for "Snowbirds and Winter Texans" who love the warm days and cool nights of the beautiful Hill Country. With no busy highways or streetlights, you can build a fire and stargaze at night, have breakfast with friendly wildlife, fish for trout, catfish or bass for your dinner, or take advantage of the nearby entertainment and shopping opportunities in Sattler, Gruene, New Braunfels or San Marcos. The Skolaut's and staff look forward to seeing and hearing from you. For information or reservations, call 830-964-3455 or visit www.lazylandl.com. *(See related story on page 12.)*

Canyon Falls RV Park is located at 14490 FM 306, on 32 lush wooded acres just 30 seconds from Canyon Lake and the Guadalupe River. The park overlooks a spring-fed creek, three ponds, a natural swimming hole and several breathtaking waterfalls for which it was named. Tim and Marian Swanson have renovated the beautiful park to include 55 RV sites with full hookups that have 30 and 50 amp service, tent sites, cabins, two comfort stations and laundry facilities. Guests can hike the nature paths, saddle up for a horseback ride through the oak tree lined trails, or float in a tube on the ponds. A kids' play area and volleyball court will keep the little ones happy for hours. Then, for kids of all ages picnic areas with BBQ grills are available. And, your pets are welcome! Fish, tube, ski or just enjoy the peace and beauty of Canyon Falls RV Park. Visit www.canyonfallsrvpark.com or call 830-214-3033.

ABBOTT'S RENTALS, INC.

Myrna Abbott invites you to be her guest on the beautiful Guadalupe River! Abbott's Rentals, 546 Riverside Path (right off of FM 306), is a wonderful place for the entire family to enjoy the beauty of Canyon Lake, the Texas Hill Country, and spend hours of fun in the water. Continuing the work that her late husband Steve began in 1982, Abbott's Rentals has fully furnished accommodations that sleep eight to 10, campsites, and a complete range of rental equipment that includes rafts, kayaks and "toobs." Be sure to float the famous "Toob Loop," (you float the loop, walk back a little ways and do it again!) The three-bedroom rentals overlook the Guadalupe River from a covered balcony and are furnished with a full kitchen, cable TV, and washer and dryer. Not overly elaborate, just great family fun in a wonderful place for kids of all ages! For information or reservations, call 830-964-2625 or visit www.abbottsriver.com.

Located between the Guadalupe River and Canyon Lake, Yogi Bear's Jellystone Park Hill Country is the perfect campground-resort for family fun. This wonderful oak-shaded property is located at 12915 FM 306 and includes RV and tenting areas, three private cottages, and 20 lodge rooms. Comfort stations, meeting rooms and recreation rooms make Jellystone the perfect place to relax with old and new friends. The cottages have full kitchens and the lodge rooms feature kitchenettes, cable TV and linens. Picnic tables (just guard your picnic basket from Yogi!), and grills are scattered throughout the park.

Whether you are an experienced RV traveler, a first-time tent camper or prefer fully furnished lodging, this is a great choice for camping fun. Guests can use the seasonal outdoor pool, heated indoor pool, spa, arcade, game room, and children's playground. Round up the family for a basketball game, sand volleyball, horseshoes or washers, or join other campers for Hey-Hey Rides with Yogi Bear, crafts and pancake breakfasts. Friday and Saturday nights you'll be entertained with the English Brother's chuck wagon supper, a cowboy music show and personal appearances by Yogi Bear himself!

With such close proximity to the water, you can take the family trout or bass fishing, swimming, sailing, parasailing, water skiing, snorkeling or scuba diving. You can also enjoy dinner cruises on the lake, horseback riding, hiking and golf. And, let's not forget fabulous shopping in the surrounding towns.

In the park, the Country Store is filled with lots of fun merchandise, gifts and souvenirs, and necessities like ice, camping items and groceries. Formerly known as the Maricopa Ranch Resort, delightful Christian owners Larry and Kim Jones have upgraded this resort, anticipating all your comforts and needs. For more information or reservations, call 830-964-5781, 877-964-3731 or visit www.jellystonehillcountry.com.

Three generations have been staying and playing at Rio Raft & Resort in Canyon Lake, where unique river fun and scenic Hill Country beauty are the perfect combination for an unforgettable family vacation. Located on the Guadalupe River, at 14130 River Rd., and just minutes from beautiful Canyon Lake, Rio Raft & Resort offers 25 cozy cabins, RV hookups, guided fishing trips, camping, swimming, tubing, rafting and, of course, breathtaking scenery. The cabins overlook the river, and all have individual decks and barbecue grills. Since 1977 this family-owned resort has been the perfect place for family reunions. You can float lazily in the river frontage, or try something more exciting like a thrilling whitewater trip or novice run. Whatever the ride, you'll love the panoramic beauty of the cypress-canopied river and green shrouded hills. Rio Raft & Resort is open year round for great fun! For more information, call 830-964-3613, 877-RIO-RAFT (746-7238) or visit www.rioraft.com.

Fashion, Accessories & Jewelry

Everyone deserves a little something special—something stylish, yet affordable. That's just what Tattered Hydrangea provides. This charming New Braunfels' boutique is located at 1190 W. San Antonio St. in a converted 1920s stone house. From the moment you walk in the door, allure and style embrace you—from the shop's original wainscoting and crystal chandeliers to the great selection of denim, ultra feminine jewelry and fabulous underwear. Tattered Hydrangea carries denim lines like 7 for All Mankind, People's Liberation, Tag+ jeans, Splendid, Puella, Language and Johnny Was. No matter your age or the occasion, owner Allison Deakin offers the latest fashions at superb prices in a warm, friendly environment. She rolls out the red carpet for her VIP customers with special gatherings and even produces fashion shows for the public. Call 830-643-0880 or visit www.tattered-hydrangea.com. Remember, you deserve it!

Two Chic Chicks

Mother daughter owners Kay and Kimberly Scott first began their shop online, but in just two short years, Two Chic Chicks has become one of the Texas Hill Country's premier all-inclusive bridal, special occasion and gift boutiques. They are an authorized Demetrios salon and carry Jody Coyote jewelry and handbags plus collectibles by Westland. Recently, they launched their own handmade fine jewelry and signature candle collections! This delightful shop is located in Spring Branch's Faithville shopping area at 17130 Hwy. 46 W. For more information, visit www.two-chic-chicks.com or call 830-885-2699. *(See related story on page 131.)*

Gruene with Envy
SPIRITED APPAREL...JEWELRY...ACCESSORIES

Nita Dixon's style and flair are evident throughout her wonderful boutique. An experienced shop owner (She used to have five stores at one time!), Nita has owned Gruene With Envy since 1999, and this shop is a stylish place to find incredible fashions, fabulous shoes and great jewelry and accessories. The store is located at 1244 Gruene Rd. in Historic Gruene in a 1900s cottage that was originally built from a Sear's catalog kit. Gruene With Envy offers fashion lines like Flax and Ivy Jane clothing, Mary Frances purses, and Yellow Box shoes. Yellow Box's trendy, casual shoes are popular with all ages, and the store's silver jewelry has a contemporary Southwestern vibe. Your friends and family are sure to be "green with envy" when they see your great fashion finds from this remarkable specialty store. Call 830-627-0612.

Cristal's
clothing • accessories • gifts

In 2000, Cristal Garrett left the corporate world to join her mom as co-owner of a boutique in Wimberley, Texas. Just a few years later she bought out her mom and opened another store, Cristal's, at Faithville in Spring Branch. (Now mom works for her!) Today, Cristal has three locations and the clothes she offers reflect her own personality, one that is sweet, spicy, fun and stylish. She carries wonderful fashion accessories and a large variety of ladies apparel, including well-known lines like Tummy Tuck Jeans and ZoZo. Each of her stores has a little different style, so you can choose which store (and style!) best reflects you. You will love the fashionable selection of clothes and the friendly, helpful staff. And even better, Cristal's is kind to your pocketbook too. Visit all three locations, 17130 Hwy. 46 W. in Spring Branch (830-885-2394); 13904 RR 12 in Wimberley (512-847-6383); and 1754 FM 2673 in Sattler (830-907-2583). *(See related story on page 131.)*

SASSY SPUR

The name fits this hip boutique and its charming owner to a Texas "T." Although Susan Bradley hails from Northern California, her Texas born and bred (NFL coach) husband introduced her to the Texas Hill Country, and she's here to stay! Her wonderful store, the Sassy Spur, 17130 Hwy. 46 W at Faithville in Spring Branch, is filled top to bottom with eclectic, unusual gifts, kitchenware, fashion accessories and Shabby Chic treasures. Susan carries fabulous painted furniture pieces from French Country to whimsical. She even offers antiques that have been refurbished with cowhide. The building itself is a treasured antique too. It was built during the early 1900s in the quaint village of Alamo Heights and moved to Spring Branch. This is a wonderful place to shop for the unusual because the store inventory changes constantly. For more information, call 830-885-4832 and don't miss Sassy Spur's clearance location at 2355 Bulverde Rd. in Bulverde (830-438-7955). *(See related story on page 131.)*

Christy's Jewelry & Treasures

Christy Sebby admits that, "The apple doesn't fall far from the tree!" When she moved away from her Georgia hometown to Texas, she decided to open a store like the ones her mom had always owned while she was growing up. Having been around the retail business all her life, she was a natural, with a great eye for the unique at wholesale markets. Christy's Jewelry & Treasures, 15551 FM 306, is a wonderful jewelry and gift boutique considered by all ages to be "fun, funky and cool!" Besides jewelry, Christy carries fabulous purses by Molly 'N Me, stylish flip flops, Western items, children's accessories and yummy candles. The store is also a favorite place to shop for the latest trends in college items, and everyone appreciates the low prices on such great merchandise. Christy's Jewelry & Treasures will become a favorite place to shop! (Mom, you trained her well!) Call 830-964-4606. *(See related story on page 132.)*

Furniture & Interior Design

C & C MERCANTILE

Warmth and richness embrace you as you enter C & C Mercantile. Just looking at the gorgeous home furnishings will make you want to relax in one of its plush chairs with a good book. Brothers Cary and Cody Caldwell are passionate about offering pieces that will last for generations. Cary has been in the furniture and interior design business since 1987, and Cody joined him a few years ago to make it a family affair. They offer an eclectic blend of furnishings—from Mesquite furniture to custom-made pieces and imports from India and Romania. Several of their items have even been featured in Texas Monthly magazine and the Neiman Marcus catalog. C & C Mercantile is located in New Braunfels at 142 W. San Antonio St. in a beautiful historical building. Call 830-626-2279.

Tish's Decor & More
"Serving all Your Decorating Needs"

With a passion for creating beautiful and relaxing living spaces, Tish Sutton and her talented design staff invite you to visit Canyon Lake's most remarkable interior design and home décor store. True Texas charm greets you at the door of Tish's Décor & More, 1642 FM 2673 in downtown Sattler. It is a unique combination of interior design and local Texas artistry, where you will discover one-of-a-kind items and custom artwork that will give your home great character and style.

Tish has many years of experience and a flair for eloquent and distinguished design, and her store is a reflection of her unique style. Tables are decorated with gorgeous collections and the rooms and walls are filled with works of art by local painters, sculptors and artisans.

Tish's Décor & More has a reputation as one of the finest interior design firms in the area, offering what Tish calls, "big city services in a small town environment." In helping design your home, no detail will be left to chance. Their services include flooring, window treatments, counter tops, upholstery, lighting, stone/cement, plumbing and interior design. From custom counter tops and crown molding to entertainment centers and faux finishes, the design team will coordinate every detail.

Need help getting ready for the holidays? The Christmas Store located within Tish's Décor & More is the perfect place for custom treatments and decorations that will set your home apart. From custom garlands to holiday lights, Tish will help deck your halls without the hassle. For more information, visit www.tishsdecor.com or call 830-964-6050.

Gifts, Home Décor & Specialty Shops

The Cottage

There are many things that make The Cottage in Gruene such a wonderful place to shop. This charming gift boutique is housed in a 133-year-old farmhouse, complete with original brick walls and a welcoming wrap-around porch and swing. Besides the great selection of quality ladies clothing and accessories, the rooms are filled to the rafters with everything from teapots and greeting cards to New Braunfels historical afghans. The main reason, however, that The Cottage is such a favorite is the personality and charm of the owner, Betty Paine. This vivacious businesswoman decided to follow her life-long dream and opened the shop at the young age of 50! Her zest for life and fun is evident throughout the store—in the whimsical teacups that hang from the ceiling and her colorful custom mosaic furniture. The Cottage is located at 1623 New Braunfels St. For more information, call 830-620-9622.

China -n- Things
Gifts • Home Décor • Ladies Fashion

Merle Brown and Pat Milam met at New Braunfels' 2002 Christmas market. Merle was promoting her beautiful gifts and home décor while Pat promoted her signature fashions. Because their booths were so close, they became each other's best customer! Merle invited Pat to host a trunk show in her shop, China-N-Things. It was so successful that the two joined forces. And now, Something Beautiful is permanently situated inside China-N-Things at 363 Landa St.

China-N-Things, a New Braunfels tradition since 1981, now embraces today's casual living. Instead of carrying china, as their name suggests, this fabulous store now offers gifts and home accents like Pandora jewelry, Arthur Court, Heartwood Creek, Tervis Tumblers and Tucci Candles. Something Beautiful offers unique women's clothing, shoes and accessories like French Dressing Jeans, San Miguel and Onesole shoes, and Spanx. It's a match made in heaven! Call 830-625-9639.

Something Beautiful
Fun Unique Fashions

Sophie's Shop
within SOPHIENBURG MUSEUM

If you love history, you'll love visiting the Sophienburg Museum, 401 W. Coll St., a delightful view into New Braunfels' German heritage. And tucked inside this fascinating museum, is Sophie's Shop, the year-round Christmas and gift store. This store is a fabulous resource for New Braunfels collectibles and the finest German and European nutcrackers, smokers, pyramids, and Christmas ornaments. Children will love the selection of old-fashion children's toys, and history buffs will find an array of books on Texas history and the area's first German settlers. Visit www.sophienburg.com or call 830-629-1572.

The Sophienburg

C&C'S SCENTCHIPS & Gifts

Sisters Cella Hunter and Cindy Flowers are the charming owners of C & C's Scentchips & Gifts, located at 172 W. San Antonio St. Scentchips are fragranced wax chips shaped like leaves and flowers. They have been handmade in Texas for more than 25 years. Cella and Cindy loved the product so much they opened this store in New Braunfels. They offer many alluring fragrances, or they can help you create your own signature scent. C & C's also carries burners and an array of very unique gifts and antiques. This wonderful shop not only smells terrific, but also has a delightful history. The 1920s building that houses it was once a men's hat shop. Let Cella and Cindy help you find the perfect gift for any occasion, and remember that gift baskets are available. Call 830-626-1777.

Stepping Stones

In 2006 Gordon and Darcy Colson left their fast-paced design careers in South Florida and slowed down to a more relaxed pace in Historic Gruene. They opened Stepping Stones Gift Shop, at 1627 New Braunfels St, in a quaint little house—next door to the River House Tea Room. Stepping Stones offers a lovely selection of enchanting gifts, beautiful home furnishings and unique accessories. One entire room is devoted to inspirational books and music as well as a variety of Christian children's products. Stepping Stones' peaceful environment welcomes you when you walk through the door. Big comfortable leather chairs invite you to relax and read for a while… It's the perfect place to take a moment for yourself or chat with Darcy, Gordon or one of their daughters. Stepping Stones also offers professional Interior Design and Architectural services. They love meeting new friends, so stop by and say hello! Call 830-625-3227 or visit www.steppingstonesgiftshop.com.

Miss Ruby is a charmer, and her remarkable store in Gruene reflects her fun-loving, effervescent personality. Miss Ruby's, 1633 Hunter RD., is a treat to shop, especially on the weekends when guests (21 and older) are treated to beer, wine and samples of Ya Ya's Gourmet Foods, (named after Miss Ruby's grandmother who gave her the recipes). Be sure to try Ya Ya's Jalapeno Pepper Jelly and Miss Ruby's Jalapeno Peanut Brittle. The store is filled with Texas gifts and home décor and garden items, fabulous jewelry, belts, crosses, purses and wonderful handmade perfumed soy candles. Be sure to call about booking Miss Ruby's Guest Haus, a three-bedroom country home just upstream from Gruene Hall. Call 830-832-8555 or visit www.missrubys.com or. *(See related story on page 144.)*

Oma's Haus Gift Shop

Oma's Haus Gift Shop opened as a small roadside shop selling sausage and food gifts. Now, it's not only known for its delicious Texas-style German food but for the wonderful gift items. This charming New Braunfels' landmark is located at 541 Hwy. 46 S, one block east of I-35. The Gift Shop features items from all over the world, including shelves and shelves of elaborate beer steins in all sizes, beautiful picture frames and plaques, stuffed animals, countless greeting cards, and a great selection of jewelry. Pick up a specialty gourmet treat as a reminder of your scrumptious meal at Oma's Haus Restaurant. You'll also find a delicious variety of homemade bakery items and an assortment of gourmet foods and delectable candies. For more information, call 830-625-3280 or visit www.omashaus.com. *(See related story on page 170.)*

"Miss Mellie's"
memoirs amor'e

Melanie Caldwell tried retirement. In fact, she tried it several times, but she just isn't the sort of person who can sit around and do nothing! Her zest for life and love of people just can't be squelched, and it's these traits that inspired her to open Miss Mellie's. Being a Canyon Lake local has helped Melanie keep her inventory current and relevant to the community's needs, wants and style. She carries many popular lines of beautiful gifts, seasonal treasures and wonderful fashion accessories. Fashion items for infants, tweens, teens and even pets are always trendy and current. Miss Mellie's carries lines such as Ganz and Avanti—we loved the unique, fun rain boots! For more information stop by Miss Mellie's at 1867 FM 2673, where Melanie says, "the heart remembers," or visit www.missmelliesamore.com or call 830-964-5656.

Lady Jane's

A sign in the store says, "Your husband called and said Buy Anything you want!" That won't be hard. You'll want everything you see in this fabulous Spring Branch gift boutique. Lady Jane's, 17130 Hwy. 46 W., is filled with fine treasures for your home and wonderful accessories for you and your wardrobe. With more than 30 years of retail experience, owner Janie Linn's eye for detail and quality is apparent throughout the store. You will find unique tabletop decorations, unusual art pieces and gilded mirrors; candleholders, candles and even jewelry. Janie fixed me up with a fabulous necklace! There is also a delightful collection of baby and children's items. Lady Jane's is located in the Faithville shopping area behind the Gathering Place. Visit www.ladyjanesfinethings.com or call 830-885-5437. *(See related story on page 131.)*

Quilts, Needlework & Stitchery

Both new and experienced quilters will love this incredible store in New Braunfels. The Quilt Haus, 651 N. Business IH-35, is filled with books and patterns for quilts, wearables, bags, and home décor items; notions, gifts, and especially fabric. From flannels to Kaffe Fassett, batiks to reproductions, children's prints to the newest colors and styles, it's all here! Owner Deanne Quill enjoys creating and publishing original quilt patterns, and features a friendly and talented staff, many of whom also teach classes in the spacious store. The Quilt Haus has a variety of great quilting kits, and maintains the best selection of Texas bluebonnet and Western fabrics in the area.

With four school-aged children, Deanne and husband Matt support school reading programs and the local guild's storybook outreach program by donating quilts and supplies. The Quilt Haus hosts the local chapter of Project Linus, which provides homemade blankets and quilts to ill and traumatized children in the area. Call 830-620-1382 or visit www.quilthaus.com.

Realtors

Scenic River Properties

Newcomers to the beautiful Texas Hill Country love the abundance of exciting opportunities that surround the Guadalupe River and Canyon Lake. And, the New Braunfels area is becoming a favorite place for second homes. Whether you are looking for a permanent or vacation home or just need a house for the weekend or summer, Bridget McDougall is the realtor to call! She has more than 22 years of diverse real estate experience and has owned Scenic River Properties at 1295 Sattler Rd. in Sattler since 1990. Bridget's knowledge of the Hill Country comes from experience. Because she grew up in the area and is familiar with all of the available real estate, she can match you to the perfect property. She also offers either short or long-term rentals of quality, fully furnished houses. For more information, visit www.scenicriverproperties.com or call 830-964-3127, 800-765-7077. *(See related story on page 149.)*

Restaurants & Tea Rooms

When a crew from ABC's Good Morning America set out on a five-state tour to find the most authentic German barbecue in the land, they ended up at Granzin Bar-B-Q, 660 W. San Antonio St. in New Braunfels. Owner Miles Granzin showed them just how it was done, and served up plates full of slow-smoked German barbecue. The New Yorkers were duly impressed! You will be too when you taste the delicious pit smoked sausage, pork ribs, ham, chicken, turkey and brisket. Granzin, which has been in business since 1984, uses only mesquite wood in the open pits, and lots of it. The meats are smoked to perfection, and served with delicious sides like baked potatoes, beans, cole slaw and, of course, German potato salad. For a Texas twist, order a chopped beef, chicken, turkey or sausage taco! The fresh baked bread and scrumptious pecan pie are brought in daily from Nagelin's Bakery—owned by Miles' brothers. Call 830-629-6615 or visit www.granzinbbq.net for all your catering and party needs. *(See related stories on pages 138 and 145.)*

 Old World charm, high ceilings, gleaming hardwood floors, a cozy fireplace and views that take your breath away... and we haven't even mentioned the food! Gruene River Grill, 1259 Gruene Rd., sits high over the Guadalupe River with an outdoor deck that offers great ambiance for dining or parties. The mouthwatering menu features delicious seafood, steaks and pastas, grilled specialties and outstanding desserts. Chef Dave Pavlock attended culinary school in New York, spent time abroad opening restaurants, and has worked in 5-Star resorts. From appetizers like the hand-rolled Shrimp Won Tons with cherry mustard sauce or the crispy flash fried calamari with two sauces to great entrees like the award-winning Hawaiian-style baby back ribs and the always-popular Balsamic Ribeye, everything on the menu is fantastic! There is an excellent wine list, and the desserts are definitely worth the wait. Gruene River Grill also specializes in hosting special events of all sizes. For more information, visit www.gruenerivergrill.com or call 830-624-2300.

 If you've ever thought all tearooms were alike, you're in for a pleasant surprise. The River House Tea Room, at 1617 New Braunfels St., offers succulent food from award-winning chef, Carol Hill. Carol had worked in the food industry for more than a decade, even teaching at a culinary school in Dallas. Then in 1997, she decided to open her own restaurant in a turn-of-the-20th century house in Historic Gruene. Five years later Carol became the second woman to receive the honor of State Chef of the Year by the Texas Chefs Association. Though the menu includes sandwiches and salads, Carol is especially proud of her soups and quiche, items that she "reinvents" on a daily basis. River House Tea Room also caters to a masculine crowd, offering dishes like Pistachio Crusted Pork Tenderloin. River House has a private party room and an outdoor area that's perfect for hosting special events. This is one tearoom, which cannot be missed. For more information, call 830-608-0690 or visit www.riverhousetearoom.net.

Gathering Place

When Darlene McIntosh retired after standing behind a hairdresser chair for 21 years, she was just getting started! Started, that is, on a new career that she knew God wanted her to embrace. Darlene had prayed for the opportunity to have her own tearoom, and she never let go of her faith in God's ability to make her dream come true. At 63 years young, she was finally able to purchase the historic 1914 home, and Gathering Place was born.

Darlene dreamed of having a tearoom that was the cornerstone for a community of shops in what she would call, Faithville. And when her daughter-in-law, Melony, partnered with her, Darlene's dream became a family affair. Today in Faithville, there are several shops and boutiques around the Tea Room that feature clothing, antiques, jewelry and home décor. There is even a beautiful chapel where visitors can listen to music, pray, light a candle or just be blessed. The McIntoshes also plan to open a Southern plantation-style bed and breakfast called Ascending Dove in late 2008.

Darlene's Tea Room gets its name from Matthew 18:20, the Bible verse that says, "For where two or three are gathered together in my name, there am I in the midst of them." The Gathering Place indeed has an atmosphere of joy and Christian love, and the food is absolutely "heavenly!"  From appetizers like Blackberry Jalapeno Ambrosia and Deep Fried Sweet Potato Strips to comforting soups, fresh salads and piled high sandwiches, everything is delicious. Save room for a dessert from the "Bread of Life Bakery," which features homemade breads, pastries, tarts and berry cobblers. Catering is also available for special events. Stop by 17130 Hwy. 46 W. in Spring Branch. Call 830-885-6388 or visit www.gatheringplaceatfaithville.com. *(See related story on page 131.)*

In 1977, Rodney Reagan was just 20 years old when he opened his small shop. That shop, Oma's Haus Restaurant, has grown into an internationally known restaurant and bakery. "We are what New Braunfels is all about," Rodney says. "Oma's food represents the mixing of Texas and German culture, which means our German Food is uniquely Texas style." Oma's Haus Restaurant, 541 Hwy. 46 S (one block east of I-35), features great selections of old world favorites like Sausage and Sauerkraut and Wiener Schnitzel. Imported beer and wines round out an unforgettable experience in the Bier Garten. From delicious recipes that have been handed down through four generations of "omas" (German for grandmas), the German dishes will appeal to the entire family. Try "The Ultimate," hand-breaded chicken or pork, topped with grilled onions, bacon and cream gravy. Then finish with a superb slice of strudel—delicious! For more information, call 830-625-3280 or visit www.omashaus.com. *(See related story on page 163.)*

Even big kids need a hangout, a place where they can spend time with other "big kids," enjoy great food and drinks and engage in their favorite activities. Scores Sports Bar & Grill offers diners a place to socialize with friends, eat, drink and merrily watch all the sports they can handle. And while men will love this place, we're sure women will enjoy it too. The building, at 223 W. San Antonio St. in New Braunfels, was built in the early 1900s as a JC Penney store. Today, its warmth embraces you as soon as you walk in the door, and the food is delicious too! Patrons enjoy 14 plasma TVs tuned into the latest sports games, two movie-style projectors, pool tables and foosball. Scores offers nightly specials like NTN trivia, Texas Hold'em and Karaoke. For more information, call 830-620-9091 or visit www.scoresportsbar-nb.com.

When Gunter and Cornelia Dirks immigrated to Texas from Germany in 2005, they were delighted to find the picturesque, historic community of New Braunfels in which to settle with their children and extended family. The town responded with equal delight when the Dirks family opened Friesenhaus Restaurant & Bakery, 148 S. Castell Ave.

Friesenhaus has become a favorite place for folks (German or not) to meet, speak German, listen to German music, and of course, enjoy delicious, authentic German food. The Dirks say, "It is more than a restaurant. It is a place with German Gemütlichkeit (warm friendliness) where people can meet with old friends or make new ones."

Great German food is prepared fresh daily, and includes breakfast, lunch and dinner. They serve up a variety of wonderful German entrees including the classic Wiener Schnitzel, Sauerbraten, Schnitzel, soups, cabbage and sausages, and don't forget to save room for the freshly baked German breads, pastries and desserts like Torten, Kuchen and Strudel.

The building has a charming European atmosphere, and includes an indoor dining room, wine bar, meeting room, ice cream parlor and Biergarten. Be sure to see the fascinating outside mural depicting the building's history. To go along with the delicious German fare, you'll also love the selection of fine German beers on draft like Hofbrau, Warsteiner and Hefeweizen.

For more information, visit www.friesenhausnb.com or call 830-625-1040.

Salons, Spas, Cosmetics, Health & Beauty

ARTQUEST PERMANENT COSMETICS

Patsy Keim, owner of ArtQuest Permanent Cosmetics, has always loved art. An artist for 30 years, she worked with oils, watercolors, acrylics and pastels. She taught art for 20 years, specializing in color theory, design, composition and drawing. It was an easy transition for her to move from art on a canvas to Permanent Cosmetic body art. She took her initial training in Permanent Makeup, Microdermabrasion, and received the Adriel Perfect Brow Design Master certification in San Antonio with international instructor, Terry Lively. Patsy then completed her advanced training in Dallas at the renowned Sandi Hammons' American Institute of Intradermal Cosmetics. Her services include Permanent Cosmetics and Body Art Tattooing, Facial Microdermabrasion, Lash Extensions, Brow/Lip Waxing, Brow Tinting, European Eye Accents and Mucosal Eyeliner. She also offers inner beauty with the Isagenix Nutritional and Weight Loss System. Located near beautiful Canyon Lake at 1500 FM 2673 in Sattler. Call 830-964-4315 or visit www.artqueststudio.com.

THE HILARIOUS HAIRDRESSER

Joanie Chappell is a vivacious Italian businesswoman that migrated her way to Sattler from the northeast. Known as the "Hilarious Hairdresser," Joanie makes sure that her customers not only look great, but that their day is just a little brighter from spending time with her. Being a cosmetologist for more than 30 years, as well as a stand-up comedian, Joanie's salon stands out from the rest because of her ability to make people look good and feel good, too (with no additional charge for the laughs). The Hilarious Hairdresser, formerly Mane Attractions, is a full-service salon and, of course, a place where laughter fills the air. Be sure and ask her about the Canyon Lake Angel Foundation, inspired by the angel at Canyon Lake. For more information, visit www.thehilarioushairdresser.com or call 830-964-4697.

HEALING HANDS MASSAGE STUDIO
And
ART GALLERY

Nestled in the peace and tranquility of Canyon Lake, far away from the hectic busyness of the world, you'll find a beautiful place to relax, rejuvenate and reconnect with nature. Treat yourself to an hour, an afternoon or a day at Healing Hands Massage Studio and Art Gallery. Owner and masseuse Lisa Ansley, R.M.T., is dedicated to providing clients with a way to restore balance to both body and soul through Swedish Relaxation Massage, which uses long smooth strokes to melt stress and tension; Reflexology, a holistic stimulation of reflex points to revitalize the body's energy; and "La Stone" Therapy Massage, a unique combination of cooled marble and heated basalt stones that increases circulation and leaves you with a sense of well being. Be sure and take time to stroll through the beautiful art gallery and labyrinth. Call 830-237-7566 for an appointment, directions or gift certificates.

BodyWerks Massage Therapy & A Great ESCAPE BathHaus SPA

She is the "Massage Therapist to the Stars," Artists/Musicians/Athletes from all around the world. Vanessa Carpenter's skilled hands have worked on The San Antonio SPURS, tennis legend John Newcombe, George Strait, Def Leppard, Josh Groban, Rascal Flatts, Aerosmith, Sammy Hager, Nickelback, and Kenny Chesney, just to name a few. She has been a registered massage therapist and instructor for 13 years and has developed a massage called Structural BodyWork that incorporates deep long flowing strokes with stretches that target the core levels of the body. Offering facials, body treatments, and massage therapy, you're in for a true experience! In keeping the romance alive Vanessa caters to couples offering classes teaching massage techniques for that special date night.

Vanessa and her trained team of therapists are available at three locations: **Bodywerks Massage Therapy** at 1633 New Braunfels St. in Gruene (830-629-3757), **A Great ESCAPE BathHaus SPA** at 295 E. San Antonio St. in New Braunfels (830-620-6800) and **BodyWerks Wellness Massage Therapy**, located inside Whole Foods Market at the Quarry in San Antonio (210-651-1700). For more information, visit www.bathhausspa.com.

Special Events, Groups & Corporate

LIVE OAK RANCH

When Jay Heck opened Live Oak Ranch in New Braunfels, he was fulfilling a life-long desire to love and serve God and to help others. This incredible full-service Christian retreat and conference center located at 1851 Ponderosa Dr., lies just off the banks of the Guadalupe River, less than 45 miles from San Antonio. Jay says, "The Holy Spirit is present in this beautiful place. We pray it is a place where individuals can get away... and find their way." The wonderful staff at the Ranch also has that same desire and it is obvious in everything that they do! Live Oak Ranch hosts Christian organizations, churches, women's and men's groups and youth ministries for ages 15 and up. The Ranch can accommodate 70 people, and comfort is a high priority. Guests can swim, tube, fish, hike through the beautiful Texas Hill Country, and play volleyball and horseshoes. Nightly bonfires create many wonderful memories, and the food is almost better than mom's! For information or reservations, call 830-964-5540 or visit www.liveoakranch.org.

On December 14, 1901, ladies and gentlemen donned their most elegant clothing and gathered for the gala opening of the Seekatz Opera House in New Braunfels. The magnificent Opera House had been the dream of brothers Louis and Otto Seekatz, who wanted to attract traveling shows and local entertainment to their hometown.

The original building featured a wooden floor with removable seating for dancing and a large stage with velvet curtains and many backdrops. The second story included beautiful balconies and private clubrooms. For 40 years the Seekatz Opera House thrived as the city's premier entertainment and social center, hosting New Year's Eve dances, traveling vaudeville shows, orchestra concerts, Firemen's Balls and elegant soirées. Old timers remember famous entertainers such as Arthur Godfrey and Sally Rand on the stage. Eventually, motion pictures became the entertainment trend and the Opera House was the place to see silent, then talking, pictures.

Unfortunately, the beautiful building succumbed to fire in 1941 but was rebuilt soon after. It had many different uses over the next 60 years until 2004, when Ron Snider and Darrell Sollberger renovated it to its present glory for its original intended use.

The Seekatz Opera House, 265 W. San Antonio St., is available for weddings, corporate events, special interest groups or elegant galas for as many as 500 guests. State-of-the-art video and digital sound capabilities allow guests to host any type of meeting or social event, and the magnificent building lends the romance of history with true elegance. This is such a popular and remarkable facility that books quickly and far in advance.

For information or reservations, call 830-643-0809 or visit www.seekatzoperahouse.com.

When Jack Turpin opened T Bar M Tennis Camp in New Braunfels in 1968, he had no idea that it would grow to be one of the nation's top sports camp, resort and conference center. In fact, T Bar M was recently named a premier destination by the *Travel Channel*. You'll find Turpin's name in the Texas Tennis Hall of Fame, and his passion for kids, sports and Christian leadership is legendary. Today, Jack enjoys visiting T Bar M and feels the joy of seeing his son Scott following in his footsteps.

The resort stretches over 160 beautiful acres, offering guests relaxing accommodations and a variety of exciting outdoor activities. No longer a Hill Country secret, T Bar M is a choice location for corporate retreats, group seminars, and weddings. Located at 2549 Hwy. 46 W. and only 30 miles from the San Antonio airport and 48 miles from the Austin airport, the Center is designed for meetings for up to 300 people. The full-service Conference Center features more than 13,000 square feet of private meeting space, 29,000 square feet for receptions and banquets, wonderful lodging accommodations and excellent food service. In fact, the dining service has won numerous awards for its delicious country breakfasts, famous soups, hot lunches, outstanding dinners and delectable desserts. Let the staff at T Bar M build a corporate package for your group that can include challenge course programs, team-building outdoor activities and a first-class fitness plan. And don't forget the barbecue and bonfires!

With the breathtaking beauty of the Texas Hill Country as a backdrop, charming cottages, tennis villas, and an interactive staff that will charm you with Texas hospitality, T Bar M is the ideal choice for your next event. For more information, call 830-625-7738, 800-292-5469 or visit www.tbarm.com. *(See related story on page 148.)*

NOTES

Index

23 Skadoo – 59
A Little Room – 31
Aaron Pancoast Carriage House – 42, VI
Abbott's River Rentals, Inc. – 152
Alamo Antique Mall – 33
Alamo City's Little Flower Inn – 40, X
Alamo Plants and Petals – 44
American Indian Jewelry Stores – 119
Aragon Spanish Academy – 58
Arbor House Suites – 41
Architectural Elements – 31
Artifacts – 82
Artquest Permanent Cosmetics – 172
Ascending Dove – 169
Austin's General Store – 132, 157
Back In The Saddle – 88
Baker's – 31
Bandera County CVB – 81
Bandera Creek Guest Cottage – 87, 93
Bandera Creek Guest House – 87, 93
Bandera General Store – 91
Barnside Lodging – 143
Baubles & Beads – 60
Bedazzled – 110
Bella Crco – 103, IV
Bill Zaner's Art Haus – 102
Bitter Creek Designs – 66
Bless Your Heart Gift Shop & Boutique – 64
BodyWerks Massage Therapy & A Great Escape BathHaus Spa – 174
Bootlegger's Fine Wines & Spirits – 75

Brauntex Performing Arts Theatre – 134
Broadway & 9th Antiques – 32
Bulverde Trading Post – 65
C & C Mercantile – 158
C & C's Scentchips & Gifts – 162
Calamity Jane's Trading Company – 112
Canyon Falls RV Park – 152
Cartouche – 31
Casa Chiapas – 50
Catrina's at the Ranch – 115, IX
Celeste – 109
China-N-Things – 161
Christy's Jewelry & Treasures – 157, 132
Cielo – 117, 107
City of Boerne – 100
Collector's Gallery – 62, X
Conservation Plaza – 137
Cristal's – 156, 131
Don Yarton Antiques – 30, 9
Downtown Antique Mall – 132
Drums' Lakeview Resort – 147, 136, XII
Enchanted Springs Ranch – 104
Encore – 60
Esther Benedict Sculptures – 83
Faithville – 131
Firefly Inn Bed & Breakfast – 140
Flying L Guest Ranch – 85
Friesenhaus Restaurant & Bakery – 171
Frontier Outfitters – 90
Garden Fantasy – 61
Gathering Place Tea Room – 169, 131
Gerlich-Wagenfuehr Haus Bed and Breakfast – 142, 137
Good & Co. – 101

INDEX **179**

Granzin Bar-B-Q – 167
Greenskeeper Inn – 141
Gruene Mansion Inn – 145
Gruene River Grill – 168
Gruene River Inn – 144
Gruene With Envy – 156
Guilott Realty, Inc. – 93, 87
Hanley-Wood – 46
Healing Hands Massage Studio and Art Gallery – 173
Hideout on the Horseshoe – 146, VIII
Hill Country Rustics – 63
Hollyhock – 113
Homestead Handcrafts – 74
Hungry Horse Restaurant – 121
Joshua Creek Ranch – 105
K Charles & Co. / Aveda Institute – 73
Kuebler Waldrip Haus & Danville Schoolhouse Bed & Breakfast – 139
La Fonda Oakhills – 70
Lady Jane's – 164, 131
Lamb's Rest Inn Bed and Breakfast – 142
Langmore Photographers – 49
Lasting Impressions (Boerne) – 117
Lasting Impressions Antiques (San Antonio) – 34
Laurie Saunders, Ltd. – 31
Lazy L & L Campground & Store – 151, 12
Leslie & Co. – 63
Lewis B. Artisan Gelato & Sorbetto Café – 133
Lindheimer House – 137
Live Oak Ranch – 175
Los Patios – 71
Madhatters Tea House & Café – 51
Medina River Guest Cottage – 87, 93

Memory Lane – 52
Miss Mellie's – 164
Miss Ruby's – 163, 144
Miss Ruby's Guest Haus – 144, 163
Mountain Breeze – 150
Naegelin's Bakery – 138, 145
Naegelins Haus Bed & Breakfast – 145, 138
Natural Bridge Caverns – 136
Natural Bridge Wildlife Ranch – 135
New Braunfels Conservation Society – 137, 142
Noble Inns – 42, VI
Off My Rocker – 29
Old Downtown Bulverde Emporium – 56
Oma's Haus Gift Shop – 163, 170
Oma's Haus Restaurant – 170, 163
Otra Vez Couture Consignment – 43
Pet Works – 48
Prince Solms Inn Bed & Breakfast – 143
Rio Raft & Resort – 154
River House Tea Room – 168
River Oak Inn and Restaurant – 92
Robin's Nest – 47
Rooms and Gardens – 31
SAS Shoe Factory and General Store – 38, IX
Sassy Spur – 157, 131
Sattler Artisans' Alley – 133, VII
Saturday Market – 45
Scenic River Properties – 149, 166
Score's Sports Bar & Grill – 170
Sculptural Designs Atelier – 36
Seekatz Opera House – 176
Shoe Biz – 88
Silver Spur Guest Ranch – 86
Something Beautiful – 161
Sophie's Shop @ The Sophienburg – 161

Spoiled Rotten Salon and Butter Beans Boutique – 94
Stepping Stones – 162
Strawmanor – XIII
Sweet Pea Cottage – 56
T Bar M Resort & Conference Center – 148, 177
Tapatio Springs Golf Resort & Conference Center – 108, 120, V
Tattered Hydrangea – 155
Texana – Land Fun Park at Lakeview Resort – 136, 147, XII
Texas Country Furniture – 84
The Alley on Main – 116
The Burlap Horse – 114
The Cave Without A Name – 106
The Cottage (Gruene) – 160
The Cottage Antiques (San Antonio) – 33
The Curious Naturalist – 74
The Faust – 148
The Flower Shop – 111
The Gallery of Lighting – 115, XII
The Gingerbread House – 89
The Green Bull Jewelry Co. – 118, XI

The Hilarious Hairdresser – 173
The Jackson House – 42, VI
The Lighthouse Coffee and Café – 69
The Love's Antiques Mall of Bandera – 82
The New Images – 72
The Ogé House – 42, VI
The Painted Plate – 57
The Quilt Haus – 165
The Rusty Bucket – 113, III
The Sophienburg – 161
The Ultimate Cheesecake Bakery – 39
The Village Gallery – 35
Tish's Décor & More – 159
Topsy Turvy – 107, 117
Two Chic Chicks – 155, 131
Villita Stained Glass – 37
Viva Rouge – 114
Yarnivore – 68
Yogi Bear's Jellystone Park Hill Country – 153

Cross Reference

Antiques
Alamo Antique Mall – 33
Artifacts – 82
Austin's General Store – 132
Broadway & 9th Antiques – 32
C & C Mercantile – 158
C & C's Scentchips & Gifts – 162
Don Yarton Antiques – 30, 9
Downtown Antique Mall – 132
Good & Co. – 101
Homestead Handcrafts – 74
Lasting Impressions Antiques (San Antonio) – 34
Leslie & Co. – 63
Off My Rocker – 29
Old Downtown Bulverde Emporium – 56
Rooms and Gardens – 31
Sassy Spur – 157
Sweet Pea Cottage – 56
The Burlap Horse – 114
The Cottage Antiques (San Antonio) – 33
The Flower Shop – 111
The Gallery of Lighting – 115, XII
The Love's Antiques Mall of Bandera – 82
The Rusty Bucket – 113, III

Artist/Art Galleries/ Photography
23 Skadoo – 59
American Indian Jewelry Stores – 119
Artquest Permanent Cosmetics – 172
Barnside Lodging – 143
Bella Creo – 103, IV
Bill Zaner's Art Haus – 102
Bitter Creek Designs – 66
C & C Mercantile – 158

Calamity Jane's Trading Company – 112
Casa Chiapas – 50
Catrina's at the Ranch – 115, IX
Don Yarton Antiques – 30, 9
Esther Benedict Sculptures – 83
Healing Hands Massage Studio and Art Gallery – 173
Hill Country Rustics – 63
Langmore Photographers – 49
Miss Mellie's – 164
Rooms and Gardens – 31
Sattler Artisans' Alley – 133, VII
Sculptural Designs Atelier – 36
Sophie's Shop – 161
Texas Country Furniture – 84
The Green Bull Jewelry Co. – 118, XI
The Love's Antiques Mall of Bandera – 82
The Painted Plate – 57
The Rusty Bucket – 113, III
The Village Gallery – 35
Tish's Décor & More – 159
Villita Stained Glass – 37

Attractions/Entertainment
Abbott's Rentals, Inc. – 152
Bill Zaner's Art Haus – 102
Brauntex Performing Arts Theatre – 134
Canyon Falls RV Park – 152
Conservation Plaza – 137
Enchanted Springs Ranch – 104
Esther Benedict Sculptures – 83
Flying L Guest Ranch – 85
Friesenhaus Restaurant & Bakery – 171
Hideout on the Horseshoe – 146, VIII
Joshua Creek Ranch – 105

Lazy L & L Campground & Store – 151, 12
Lindheimer House – 137
Mountain Breeze – 150
Natural Bridge Caverns – 136
Natural Bridge Wildlife Ranch – 135
New Braunfels Conservation Society – 137, 142
SAS Shoe Factory and General Store – 38, IX
Scores Sports Bar & Grill – 170
Seekatz Opera House – 176
Silver Spur Guest Ranch – 86
Texana – Land Fun Park at Lakeview Resort – 136, XII
The Cave Without A Name – 106
The Faust – 148
The Hilarious Hairdresser – 173
The Lighthouse Coffee & Café – 69
The Sophienburg – 161

Bakeries
Friesenhaus Restaurant & Bakery – 171
Gathering Place Tea Room – 169
Naegelin's Bakery – 138
Oma's Haus Restaurant – 170
The Ultimate Cheesecake Bakery – 39

Bed & Breakfasts/Cabins/ Cottages
Abbott's Rentals, Inc. – 152
Alamo City's Little Flower Inn – 40, X
Arbor House Suites – 41
Ascending Dove – 169
Bandera Creek Guest Cottage – 87
Bandera Creek Guest House – 87
Barnside Lodging – 143
Canyon Falls RV Park – 152

Drums' Lakeview Resort – 147, XII
Enchanted Springs Ranch – 104
Firefly Inn Bed & Breakfast – 140
Gerlich-Wagenfuehr Bed and Breakfast – 142
GreensKeeper Inn – 141
Gruene Mansion Inn – 145
Gruene River Inn – 144
Hideout on the Horseshoe – 146, VIII
Joshua Creek Ranch – 105
Kuebler Waldrip Haus & Danville Schoolhouse Bed & Breakfast – 139
Lamb's Rest Inn Bed & Breakfast – 142
Medina River Guest Cottage – 87
Miss Ruby's Guest Haus – 144
Mountain Breeze – 150
Naegelins Haus Bed & Breakfast – 145
Noble Inns – 42. VI
    –Aaron Pancoast Carriage House
    –The Jackson House
    –The Ogé House
Prince Solms Inn Bed & Breakfast – 143
Rio Raft & Resort – 154
Scenic River Properties – 149, 166
Silver Spur Guest Ranch – 86
Strawmanor – XIII
The Faust – 148
Yogi Bear's Jellystone Park Hill Country – 153

Books
SAS Shoe Factory and General Store – 38, IX
Sophie's Shop – 161
Stepping Stones – 162
The Lighthouse Coffee & Café – 69

CROSS REFERENCE **183**

Bridal/Weddings

Alamo City's Little Flower Inn – 40, X
Alamo Plants and Petals – 44
Arbor House Suites – 41
Artquest Permanent Cosmetics – 172
Collector's Gallery – 62, X
Enchanted Springs Ranch – 104
Firefly Inn Bed & Breakfast – 140
Flying L Guest Ranch – 85
GreensKeeper Inn – 141
Gruene River Grill – 168
Hanley-Wood – 46
Hideout on the Horseshoe – 146, VIII
K Charles & Co. / Aveda Institute – 73
Kuebler Waldrip Haus & Danville Schoolhouse Bed & Breakfast – 139
Lamb's Rest Inn Bed & Breakfast – 142
Langmore Photographers – 49
Miss Ruby's Guest Haus – 144
Naegelin's Bakery – 138
New Braunfels Conservation Society – 137
Noble Inns – 42, VI
Oma's Haus Restaurant – 170
Prince Solms Inn Bed & Breakfast – 143
Robin's Nest – 47
Seekatz Opera House – 176
Tapatio Springs Golf Resort & Conference Center – 108, 120, V
The Faust – 148
The Gingerbread House – 89
The Ultimate Cheesecake Bakery – 39
Two Chic Chicks – 155

Camping/RVing

Abbott's Rentals, Inc. – 152
Canyon Falls RV Park – 152
Lazy L & L Campground & Store – 151, 12
Mountain Breeze – 150
Rio Raft & Resort – 154
Yogi Bear's Jellystone Park Hill Country – 153

Catering

Flying L Guest Ranch – 85
Gathering Place Tea Room – 169
Granzin Bar-B-Q – 167
Hungry Horse Restaurant – 121
La Fonda Oakhills – 70
Los Patios – 71

Children's

Aragon Spanish Academy – 58
Bandera General Store – 91
Canyon Falls RV Park – 152
Christy's Jewelry & Treasures – 157
Collector's Gallery – 62, X
Joshua Creek Ranch – 105
Lady Jane's – 164
Miss Mellie's – 164
Natural Bridge Caverns – 136
Natural Bridge Wildlife Ranch – 135
Oma's Haus Gift Shop – 153
SAS Shoe Factory and General Store – 38, IX
Texana – Land Fun Park at Lakeview Resort – 136, XII
The Painted Plate – 57
Topsy Turvy – 107
Yogi Bear's Jellystone Park Hill Country – 153

Coffee
Casa Chiapas – 50
Lewis B. Artisan Gelato &
  Sorbetto Café – 133
Sattler Artisans' Alley – 133, VII
The Lighthouse Coffee & Café
  – 69

Condominiums/Resorts/Rentals
Abbott's Rentals, Inc. – 152
Bandera Creek Guest Cottage – 87
Bandera Creek Guest House – 87
Drums' Lakeview Resort – 147, XII
Flying L Guest Ranch – 85
Guilott Realty, Inc. – 93
Hideout on the Horseshoe – 146,
  VIII
Joshua Creek Ranch – 105
Medina River Guest Cottage – 87
Noble Inns – 42, VI
Rio Raft & Resort – 154
River Oak Inn and Restaurant – 92
Scenic River Properties – 149, 166
Silver Spur Guest Ranch – 86
Strawmanor – XIII
T Bar M Resort & Conference
  Center – 148, 177
Tapatio Springs Golf Resort &
  Conference Center – 108,120, V
Yogi Bear's Jellystone Park Hill
  Country – 153

Cosmetics/Health & Beauty Products
Artquest Permanent Cosmetics
  – 172
BodyWerks Massage Therapy &
  A Great Escape BathHaus Spa
  – 174
Healing Hands Massage Studio
  and Art Gallery – 173
K Charles & Co. / Aveda Institute
  – 73

The New Images – 72

Fashion/Accessories
23 Skadoo – 59
American Indian Jewelry Stores
  – 119
Back in the Saddle – 88
Bandera General Store – 91
Baubles & Beads – 60
Bedazzled – 110
Bitter Creek Designs – 66
Bless Your Heart Gift Shop &
  Boutique – 64
Celeste – 109
China-N-Things – 161
Christy's Jewelry & Treasures
  – 157
Collector's Gallery – 62, X
Cristal's – 156
Encore – 60
Frontier Outfitters – 90
Gruene With Envy – 156
Homestead Handcrafts – 74
Lady Jane's – 164
Miss Mellie's – 164
Miss Ruby's – 163
Otra Vez Couture Consignment
  – 43
SAS Shoe Factory and General
  Store – 38, IX
Sassy Spur – 157
Shoe Biz – 88
Something Beautiful – 161
Spoiled Rotten Salon and Butter
  Beans Boutique – 94
Tattered Hydrangea – 155
The Alley on Main – 116
The Cottage (Gruene) – 160
The New Images – 72
Two Chic Chicks – 155
Viva Rouge – 114
Yarnivore – 68

Fishing
Canyon Falls RV Park – 152
Flying L Guest Ranch – 85
Joshua Creek Ranch – 105
Lazy L & L Campground & Store
  – 151, 12
Mountain Breeze – 150
Rio Raft & Resort – 154

Florists
Alamo Plants and Petals – 44
Cielo – 117
Leslie & Co. – 63
Saturday Market – 45
The Flower Shop – 111
The Gingerbread House – 89

Furniture
Artifacts – 82
Broadway & 9th Antiques – 32
Bulverde Trading Post – 65
C & C Mercantile – 158
Calamity Jane's Trading Company
  – 112
Catrina's at the Ranch – 115, IX
Don Yarton Antiques – 30, 9
Downtown Antique Mall – 132
Frontier Outfitters – 90
Good & Co. – 101
Hill Country Rustics – 63
Lasting Impressions (Boerne)
  – 117
Lasting Impressions Antiques (San
  Antonio) – 34
Off My Rocker – 29
Old Downtown Bulverde
  Emporium – 56
Robin's Nest – 47
Rooms and Gardens – 31
Sassy Spur – 157
Stepping Stones – 162
Texas Country Furniture – 84

The Alley on Main – 116
The Burlap Horse – 114
The Cottage Antiques (San
  Antonio) – 33
The Gallery of Lighting – 115, XII
The Rusty Bucket – 113, III
Viva Rouge – 114

Gardens/Nurseries
Bulverde Trading Post – 65
Garden Fantasy – 61
Good & Co. – 101
Rooms and Gardens – 31
The Curious Naturalist – 74
The Gallery of Lighting – 115, XII

Gifts/Home Décor
23 Skadoo – 59
Alamo Plants and Petals – 44
Back in the Saddle – 88
Bandera General Store – 91
Bill Zaner's Art Haus – 102
Bless Your Heart Gift Shop &
  Boutique – 64
BodyWerks Massage Therapy &
  A Great Escape BathHaus Spa
  – 174
Broadway & 9th Antiques – 32
Bulverde Trading Post – 65
C & C Mercantile – 158
C & C's Scentchips & Gifts – 162
Calamity Jane's Trading Company
  – 112
Casa Chiapas – 50
Catrina's at the Ranch – 115, IX
Celeste – 109
China-N-Things – 161
Cielo – 117
Collector's Gallery – 62, X
Cristal's – 156
Don Yarton Antiques – 30, 9
Downtown Antique Mall – 132

Flying L Guest Ranch – 85
Frontier Outfitters – 90
Garden Fantasy – 61
Good & Co. – 101
Hanley-Wood – 46
Hill Country Rustics – 63
Hollyhock – 113
Homestead Handcrafts – 74
Lady Jane's – 164
Lasting Impressions (Boerne)
    – 117
Lasting Impressions Antiques (San
    Antonio) – 34
Leslie & Co. – 63
Madhatters Tea House & Café – 51
Memory Lane – 52
Miss Mellie's – 164
Miss Ruby's – 163
Off My Rocker – 29
Old Downtown Bulverde
    Emporium – 56
Oma's Haus Gift Shop – 163
Robin's Nest – 47
Rooms and Gardens – 31
Sassy Spur – 157
Sattler Artisans' Alley – 133, VII
Saturday Market – 45
Sculptural Designs Atelier – 36
Something Beautiful – 161
Sophie's Shop – 161
Stepping Stones – 162
Sweet Pea Cottage – 56
Tattered Hydrangea – 155
The Alley on Main – 116
The Burlap Horse – 114
The Cottage (Gruene) – 160
The Cottage Antiques (San
    Antonio) – 33
The Curious Naturalist – 74
The Flower Shop – 111
The Gallery of Lighting – 115, XII
The Gingerbread House – 89

The Green Bull Jewelry Co. – 118,
    XI
The Lighthouse Coffee & Café – 69
The Love's Antiques Mall of
    Bandera – 82
The Painted Plate – 57
The Quilt Haus – 165
The Rusty Bucket – 113, III
The Village Gallery – 35
Tish's Décor & More – 159
Topsy Turvy – 107
Two Chic Chicks – 155
Viva Rouge – 114

Golf
Flying L Guest Ranch – 85
GreensKeeper Inn – 141
Tapatio Springs Golf Resort &
    Conference Center – 108, 120, V

Gourmet/Specialty Foods
Austin's General Store – 132
Bootlegger's Fine Wines & Spirits
    – 74
Miss Ruby's – 163
Naegelin's Bakery – 138
Oma's Haus Gift Shop – 163

Hotels/Inns
Alamo City's Little Flower Inn
    – 40, X
Drums' Lakeview Resort – 147, XII
Gruene Mansion Inn – 145
Gruene River Inn – 144
Joshua Creek Ranch – 105
River Oak Inn and Restaurant – 92
Silver Spur Guest Ranch – 86
T Bar M Resort & Conference
    Center – 148, 177
Tapatio Springs Golf Resort &
    Conference Center – 108, 120, V
The Faust – 148

Ice Cream Parlor
Lewis B. Artisan Gelato & Sorbetto Café – 63
SAS Shoe Factory and General Store – 38, IX

Interior Design
A Little Room – 31
Alamo Antique Mall – 33
Architectural Elements – 31
Artifacts – 82
Baker's – 31
C & C Mercantile – 158
Calamity Jane's Trading Company – 112
Cartouche – 31
Catrina's at the Ranch – 115, IX
Don Yarton Antiques – 30, 9
Frontier Outfitters – 90
Laurie Saunders, Ltd. – 31
Rooms and Gardens – 31
Stepping Stones – 162
Texas Country Furniture – 84
The Burlap Horse – 114
The Gallery of Lighting – 115, XII
The Rusty Bucket – 113, III
Tish's Décor & More – 159
Viva Rouge – 114

Jewelry
Alamo Antique Mall – 33
American Indian Jewelry Stores – 119
Back in the Saddle – 88
Baubles & Beads – 60
Bedazzled – 110
Bella Creo – 103, IV
Bitter Creek Designs – 66
Bless Your Heart Gift Shop & Boutique – 64
Broadway & 9th Antiques – 32
Bulverde Trading Post – 65
Celeste – 109

China-N-Things – 161
Christy's Jewelry & Treasures – 157
Cielo – 117
Cristal's – 156
Flying L Guest Ranch – 85
Gruene With Envy – 156
Hollyhock – 113
Homestead Handcrafts – 74
Lady Jane's – 164
Lasting Impressions (Boerne) – 117
Miss Ruby's – 163
Oma's Haus Gift Shop – 163
Otra Vez Couture Consignment – 43
Sassy Spur – 157
Shoe Biz – 88
Something Beautiful – 161
Spoiled Rotten Salon and Butter Beans Boutique – 94
Stepping Stones – 162
Tattered Hydrangea – 155
The Cottage (Gruene) – 160
The Green Bull Jewelry Co. – 118, XI
The Love's Antiques Mall of Bandera – 82
The Village Gallery – 35
Two Chic Chicks – 155
Villita Stained Glass – 37
Viva Rouge – 114

Museums
Conservation Plaza – 137
Lindheimer House – 137
New Braunfels Conservation Society – 137
The Sophienburg – 161

Pampered Pets
Hollyhock – 113
Miss Mellie's – 164
Pet Works – 48
Sweet Pea Cottage – 56

Quilts/Needlework/Stitchery
Cielo – 117
Homestead Handcrafts – 74
Memory Lane – 52
The Quilt Haus – 165
Yarnivore – 68

Realtors
Guilott Realty, Inc. – 93
Scenic River Properties – 166

Restaurants
Casa Chiapas – 50
Flying L Guest Ranch – 85
Friesenhaus Restaurant & Bakery
  – 171
Gathering Place Tea Room – 169
Granzin Bar-B-Q – 167
Gruene River Grill – 168
Hungry Horse Restaurant – 121
Joshua Creek Ranch – 105
La Fonda Oakhills – 70
Los Patios – 71
Madhatters Tea House & Café – 51
Oma's Haus Restaurant – 170
River House Tea Room – 168
River Oak Inn and Restaurant – 92
Scores Sports Bar & Grill – 170
Tapatio Springs Golf Resort &
  Conference Center – 108, 120, V
The Lighthouse Coffee & Café
  – 69

Salons/Spas/Indulgence
Artquest Permanent Cosmetics
  – 172
BodyWerks Massage Therapy &
  A Great Escape BathHaus Spa
  – 174
Healing Hands Massage Studio
  and Art Gallery – 173
K Charles & Co. / Aveda Institute
  – 73

Spoiled Rotten Salon and Butter
  Beans Boutique – 94
The Hilarious Hairdresser – 173
The New Images – 72

Soda Fountains
Bandera General Store – 91
SAS Shoe Factory and General
  Store – 38, IX

Special Events/Groups/Corporate
Abbott's Rentals, Inc. – 152
Alamo City's Little Flower Inn
  – 40, X
Alamo Plants and Petals – 44
Arbor House Suites – 41
Barnside Lodging – 143
Bitter Creek Designs – 66
BodyWerks Massage Therapy &
  A Great Escape BathHaus Spa
  – 174
Brauntex Performing Arts Theatre
  – 134
Canyon Falls RV Park – 152
Drums' Lakeview Resort – 147, XII
Enchanted Springs Ranch – 104
Faithville – 131
Firefly Inn Bed & Breakfast – 140
Flying L Guest Ranch – 85
Friesenhaus Restaurant & Bakery
  – 171
Gathering Place Tea Room – 169
Gerlich-Wagenfuehr Bed and
  Breakfast – 142
Granzin Bar-B-Q – 167
GreensKeeper Inn – 141
Gruene Mansion Inn – 145
Gruene River Grill – 168
Gruene River Inn – 144
Hideout on the Horseshoe – 146,
  VIII
Hungry Horse Restaurant – 121
Joshua Creek Ranch – 105

Kuebler Waldrip Haus & Danville Schoolhouse Bed & Breakfast – 139
La Fonda Oakhills – 70
Lamb's Rest Inn Bed & Breakfast – 142
Langmore Photographers – 49
Lazy L & L Campground & Store – 151, 12
Live Oak Ranch – 175
Los Patios – 71
Miss Ruby's Guest Haus – 144
Naegelin's Bakery – 138
Naegelins Haus Bed & Breakfast – 145
Natural Bridge Caverns – 136
Natural Bridge Wildlife Ranch – 135
Noble Inns – 42, VI
Oma's Haus Restaurant – 170
Prince Solms Inn Bed & Breakfast – 143
River House Tea Room – 168
SAS Shoe Factory and General Store – 38, IX
Saturday Market – 45
Scenic River Properties – 149, 166
Scores Sports Bar & Grill – 170
Sculptural Designs Atelier – 36
Seekatz Opera House – 176
Silver Spur Guest Ranch – 86
Strawmanor – XIII
T Bar M Resort & Conference Center – 148, 177
Tapatio Springs Golf Resort & Conference Center – 108, 120. V
Tattered Hydrangea – 155
Texana – Land Fun Park at Lakeview Resort – 136, XII
The Cave Without A Name – 106
The Faust – 148
The Hilarious Hairdresser – 173
The Painted Plate – 57

The Sophienburg – 161
The Ultimate Cheesecake Bakery – 39
Yogi Bear's Jellystone Park Hill Country – 153

Specialty Shops
American Indian Jewelry Stores – 119
Austin's General Store – 132
Bedazzled – 110
Bella Creo – 103, IV
Bootlegger's Fine Wines & Spirits – 75
C & C's Scentchips & Gifts – 162
Cielo – 117
Collector's Gallery – 62, X
Encore – 60
Garden Fantasy – 61
Gruene With Envy – 156
Hanley-Wood – 46
Hollyhock – 113
Homestead Handcrafts – 74
Lasting Impressions (Boerne) – 117
Los Patios – 71
Memory Lane – 52
Miss Mellie's – 164
Off My Rocker – 29
Otra Vez Couture Consignment – 43
Pet Works – 48
Sassy Spur – 157
Sattler Artisans' Alley – 133, VII
Saturday Market – 45
Sculptural Designs Atelier – 36
Sophie's Shop – 161
The Cave Without A Name – 106
The Cottage (Gruene) – 160
The Curious Naturalist – 74
The Gallery of Lighting – 115, XII
The Green Bull Jewelry Co. – 118, XI
The Painted Plate – 57

The Quilt Haus – 165
Tish's Décor & More – 159
Topsy Turvy – 107
Two Chic Chicks – 155
Villita Stained Glass – 37
Yarnivore – 68

Sports/Fitness
Abbott's Rentals, Inc. – 152
Canyon Falls RV Park – 152
Joshua Creek Ranch – 105
Lazy L & L Campground & Store
    – 151, 12
Mountain Breeze – 150
Rio Raft & Resort – 154
Scores Sports Bar & Grill – 170
T Bar M Resort & Conference
    Center – 148, 177

Tea Rooms
Gathering Place Tea Room – 169
Madhatters Tea House & Café
    – 51
River House Tea Room – 168

Value
Baubles & Beads – 60
Encore – 60
Otra Vez Couture Consignment
    – 43

Wines/Winery
Bootlegger's Fine Wines & Spirits
    – 75
Friesenhaus Restaurant & Bakery
    – 171
Gruene River Grill – 168
Oma's Haus Restaurant – 170

Dear Adventurer,

If you are reading this book chances are you are an 'Adventurer.' An 'Adventurer' is a person with a sense of adventure and a curiosity for new and exciting places, people and experiences—both long and short distances. All of the Lady's Day Out books appeal to that sense of adventure and cater to the natural curiosity in all of us.

A Lady's Day Out, Inc., would like to share this gift of the perfect combination between work and travel with our loyal following of readers.

In an effort to expand our coverage area we are looking for adventurous travelers who would like to help us find the greatest places to include in our upcoming editions of A Lady's Day Out. This is a wonderful opportunity to travel and explore some of the best destination cities in the United States.

If you would like more information, we would love to hear from you. You may call A Lady's Day Out, Inc. at 1-888-860-ALDO (2536) or e-mail us through www.aladysdayout.com.

Best wishes and keep on exploring, from all of us at A Lady's Day Out, Inc.

Dear Entrepreneur,

If you would like to be a business partner or owner of A Lady's Day Out, Inc., please call so we can chat. After many years of traveling and exploring, the time to pass the torch is approaching. For just the right person or group, we will be considering offers to carry on the Legacy that Paula Ramsey has trusted to our care. Call 1-888-860-ALDO (2536) or 817-236-5250 if you are interested.

Thank you,
Jennifer Ramsey

"A Lady's Day Out Giveaway"
Entry Form

Have five of the businesses featured in this book sign your entry form and you are eligible to win one of the following: weekend get away at a bed and breakfast, dinner gift certificates, shopping spree gift certificates or $250 cash.

1. _____
    (NAME OF BUSINESS)   (SIGNATURE)

2. _____
    (NAME OF BUSINESS)   (SIGNATURE)

3. _____
    (NAME OF BUSINESS)   (SIGNATURE)

4. _____
    (NAME OF BUSINESS)   (SIGNATURE)

5. _____
    (NAME OF BUSINESS)   (SIGNATURE)

NAME: _____

ADDRESS: _____

CITY: _____ STATE: _____ ZIP: _____

PHONE#: _____ E – MAIL: _____

Where did you purchase book? _____

Other towns or businesses you feel should be incorporated in our next book.

_____

_____

No purchase necessary. Winners will be determined by random drawing from all complete entries received. Winners will be notified by phone and/or mail.

Mail To:
A Lady's Day Out, Inc.
8551 Boat Club Road #117
Fort Worth, Tx 76179

Fax To: 817-236-0033
Phone: 817-236-5250
Web-Site: www.aladysdayout.com